GARY LINEKER'S
SOCCER QUIZ BOOK

GARY LINEKER'S
SOCCER QUIZ BOOK

GARY LINEKER
with William Walker

CollinsWillow
An Imprint of HarperCollins*Publishers*

This edition published in 1996 by
CollinsWillow
an imprint of HarperCollins*Publishers*
London

˙ 3 5 7 9 8 6 4 2

A CIP catalogue record for this book
is available from the British Library

ISBN 0 00 218721 3

Printed and bound in Great Britain by
Caledonian International Book Manufacturing Ltd,
Glasgow

CONTENTS

INTERNATIONAL SOCCER

MOVES, MANAGERS AND MORE

A QUIZ FOR ALL SEASONS

EUROPEAN FOOTBALL

SOCCER TRIVIA

INTRODUCTION

Football is fun. Scoring goals gave me an unbelievable buzz and nowadays I still get great enjoyment from covering matches for TV and radio.

I'm certainly confident that this brand new edition of my soccer quiz book will provide some tremendous off-field fun for you.

We've included lots of up-to-date questions covering the usual broad range of soccer topics. For example, you can back-track over recent seasons or take an inquisitive look at European or world football.

And as before, we've graded each quiz into three parts:

Open Goal (a gilt-edged opportunity to open your account)

Half-Chance (more experience needed here)

Long-Range Shot (difficult, but worth a speculative try)

There's also the special Sharp in the Box teaser to keep you on your toes.

So enjoy the challenge and keep in mind one of the golden rules of striking – if you find yourself off-target, just pick yourself up and be ready for the next one that comes along!

QUIZ 1

THE PREMIERSHIP

'In terms of pure entertainment, the English Premiership can justifiably claim to be one of the most exciting leagues in world football.'

Open Goal

1. Which team led the Premiership table for most of 1995-96 but finished as runners-up?
2. 'Stan the Man' hit 22 League goals for Nottingham Forest in his first Premiership season and 14 for Liverpool in his second. Who is he?
3. Which team did Manchester United trounce 9-0 in March 1995?
4. Who was the first player to notch 100 Premiership goals?
5. Which club began the 1994-95 season with a six-point handicap?
6. Matt Le Tissier was which club's top scorer in the first three seasons of the Premiership?

Half-Chance

7. Which team finished third in 1995-96?
8. How many London clubs are taking part in the 1996-97 Premiership?
9. Which team recorded the highest-ever Premiership away victory when they won 7-1 at Sheffield Wednesday on 1st April 1995?
10. Doug Ellis is chairman of which Midlands club?
11. At which ground did Manchester United clinch the 1996 Championship title?

12. Who did Ruud Gullit succeed as boss of Chelsea?

Long-Range Shot
13. Which club conceded the most goals in the 1995-96 Premiership?
14. Who is the Chief Executive of the FA Premier League?
15. Name the 46-year-old who was named as a substitute for West Ham against Newcastle in March '96?
16. Which Premiership player was credited with the most goal 'assists' in 1995-96?
17. Who scored the first-ever Premier League goal in August 1992?
18. How many goals were scored in the '95-96 Premiership – 988, 1088 or 1188?

Sharp in the Box
Three strikers hit Premiership hat-tricks on 23rd September 1995. Name any of the men concerned.

QUIZ 2

UPS AND DOWNS

'While at Leicester, I experienced both promotion and relegation in successive seasons. Going up is definitely a better feeling than going down!'

Open Goal
1. Who won the 1996 First Division play-offs?
2. Which team were relegated on the last day of 1995-96, having topped the First Division table earlier in the season?
3. Who guided Sunderland to promotion as the 1996 First Division champions?
4. How many teams were relegated from the Premiership in '95-96?
5. Which two Premiership teams avoided relegation on goal difference?
6. True or false – Manchester United have not been relegated during the last 25 years?

Half-Chance
7. On the last Saturday of the 1993-94 season, Everton defeated which team 3-2 to secure their Premiership survival?
8. Which team took part in the Second Division play-offs in four separate seasons between 1987 and 1992?
9. Which team won promotion in 1991 after spending 17 consecutive seasons in the old Division Two?
10. Who won the 1996 Division Three play-offs?
11. Which was the first club to suffer automatic relegation from the Football League?

12. Who led Swindon Town to successive promotions in 1986 and 1987?

Long-Range Shot
13. Which was the first club to have their relegation confirmed in 1995-96?
14. In which season did the League introduce 'three-up and three-down' between the old Divisions One and Two?
15. What were the 19th century version of the play-offs called?
16. Which founder member club was forced to seek re-election to the Football League in 1986?
17. Who made three successive play-off appearances with Blackburn, West Bromwich Albion and Wycombe between 1992 and 1994?
18. What was rather surprising about Manchester City's relegation in 1937-38?

Sharp in the Box
Three teams have won the English League Championship in the season following promotion. Can you name them?

QUIZ 3

THE FA CUP

*'Winning the FA Cup with Spurs was a real highlight
of my career – it's every footballer's dream to play
in a cup-winning team at Wembley.'*

Open Goal

1. Eric Cantona fired Manchester United's winner in the 1996 Final. Did the goal come in the first or second half?
2. Which striker has scored more Wembley FA Cup Final goals than any other player?
3. Only one FA Cup Final has ended with a result of 3–3. Can you name the teams involved?
4. Who was the goalkeeper and captain of Wimbledon in 1988?
5. Name either of the beaten semi-finalists in 1996.
6. Which was the last team to win the Cup after a replayed Final?

Half-Chance

7. Can you name the manager who led QPR to Wembley in 1982?
8. Which First Division team knocked Arsenal out of the 1996 competition?
9. Who scored an FA Cup Final winner against Everton in 1985 and later played for the Goodison Park club?
10. Which member of Sunderland's defeated side of 1992 had been a loser on three previous occasions?
11. Which was the first top division team to go out of the FA Cup on a penalty shoot-out?

12. Since 1914, Liverpool have scored fourteen goals in ten FA Cup Final appearances. How many of them were scored in the first half?

Long-Range Shot
13. What was the unusual scoreline in the second round replay between Walsall and Torquay in December 1995?
14. Which team made history by arriving at Wembley by helicopter in 1983?
15. Who refereed the 1996 Final?
16. The rival managers in the 1973 Sunderland-Leeds Final had earlier been opponents as players in the Newcastle-Manchester City match of 1955. Can you name them?
17. Since the war, only three teams have contested the FA Cup Final without an international player in their ranks. Who were they?
18. Which Arsenal defender committed an infamous 'professional foul' on West Ham's Paul Allen in the 1980 Final?

Sharp in the Box
Five post-war Manchester United managers have led The Reds to an FA Cup Final. Name them.

QUIZ 4

TO HULL AND BACK

'Although the standard may not be as high as in the top flight, the lower divisions in England are every bit as fiercely contested.'

Open Goal
1. Which Lancashire club won the Endsleigh League Third Division in 1995-96?
2. Stanley Matthews won an FA Cup medal in the tangerine shirt of this seaside club in 1953.
3. Can you name the 1964 European Footballer of the Year who began his League career with Huddersfield Town?
4. At which club did both Kevin Keegan and Ray Clemence make their debut in professional football?
5. Which BBC pundit is the chairman of Fulham?
6. Which was the highest-placed Welsh club in the 1995-96 Football League?

Half-Chance
7. Can you name the Nigerian international who is Leyton Orient's most-capped player?
8. Which South Yorkshire club have Maurice Setters, Lawrie McMenemy and Billy Bremner all managed?
9. Name the 66-year-old Football League club which folded in 1992.
10. Why are Chesterfield known as 'The Spireites'?
11. How are table positions decided when two teams are level on points in the Nationwide League?

12. Which Irish international striker netted 78 goals in 219 Football League outings for Gillingham between 1981 and 1987?

Long-Range Shot
13. Which team set a new record for consecutive seasons in the old Division Four between 1967 and 1985?
14. Can you name the former Wimbledon manager who has been in charge of Crewe since 1982?
15. Steve White hit 29 League goals for which club in 1995-96?
16. Which is the largest city in England never to have staged top division football?
17. Which Cheshire club were managed by a Uruguayan between 1989 and 1995?
18. What were Oxford United known as until 1960?

Sharp in the Box
Can you name the six British senior League clubs called 'Rovers'?

Quiz 5

Scottish Football

'Scottish football seems to have a higher profile now as clubs there bring in big names to try to keep pace with Rangers.'

Open Goal
1. Who is the Scottish Premier League's leading goalscorer of all time?
2. Which team crashed 5-1 to Rangers in the 1996 Scottish Cup Final?
3. At which club did Alex McLeish succeed Tommy McLean as manager in the summer of 1994?
4. Which Scottish team made their debut in European competition during 1995-96?
5. What are the colours of Dundee United?
6. Can you name the Glasgow-based club relegated from the Premier League in 1996?

Half-Chance
7. Who did Roy Aitken succeed as Aberdeen manager?
8. For which team did Manchester United boss Alex Ferguson once appear in a Scottish Cup Final?
9. Who were the 1996 Scottish Second Division Champions?
10. How many Scottish League clubs are there in total?
11. The town of Paisley is home to which club?
12. Who were the last pair of brothers to play together in a Scottish Cup winning team?

Long-Range Shot

13. Which provincial club won the Scottish League Championship in 1965?

14. Can you name the two Ukrainians who played for Rangers' 'Double' winning side of 1991-92?

15. Which Scottish club do pop duo The Proclaimers follow?

16. Who is the only Hearts player to have won the Scottish Footballer of the Year award?

17. With which club did Charlie Nicholas win a Scottish Cup winners medal?

18. Name the former Spanish League star who guided East Fife to promotion in 1996.

Sharp in the Box
What are the four Scottish League clubs whose name begins with the letter 'C'?

Quiz 6

The League Cup

*'Although it has never upstaged the FA Cup,
the League Cup competition has provided
many dramatic moments over the years.'*

Open Goal
1. Aston Villa defeated Leeds to lift the 1996 Coca-Cola Cup. What was the score in the Final?
2. Which was the first team to win the tournament under its present name?
3. Which manager has steered both Aston Villa and Sheffield Wednesday to League Cup success in the 1990s?
4. Who was Liverpool's two-goal hero in the 1995 Coca-Cola Cup Final?
5. Which team played in the Final in three out of the four years from 1989 to 1992?
6. Who won a record fifth League Cup medal in 1995?

Half-Chance
7. Who was ordered off in the 1996 Arsenal v Newcastle quarter-final at Highbury?
8. Sky Sports' Andy Gray scored the only goal of the 1980 League Cup Final. Which team was he playing for at that time?
9. Can you name the American international who won a League Cup medal in 1991?
10. Which ground staged League Cup Final replays in 1977 and 1978?

11. Who scored twelve goals for Spurs in the 1986-87 competition?

12. Can you remember the beaten semi-finalists in 1995-96?

Long-Range Shot

13. Which former Football League secretary is credited with originating the League Cup tournament?

14. Which Fourth Division team reached the Final in 1962?

15. Who was Chelsea manager when the Blues won the League Cup in 1965?

16. Bertie Auld, a European Cup winner with Celtic in 1967, had earlier won a League Cup medal with which club?

17. Why did the 1993 Coca-Cola Cup Final finish with a let-down for goal hero Steve Morrow?

18. In September 1995, William Hill were giving odds of 125-1 for Luton to win the Coca-Cola Cup. Why did they represent poor value?

Sharp in the Box
Between 1961 and 1996, five clubs from outside the top division lifted the League Cup. Can you name them?

QUIZ 7

OTHER TOURNAMENTS

*'There seems to be more tournaments than ever
nowadays. At least they give smaller clubs
the chance of picking up honours.'*

Open Goal

1. Which two teams traditionally compete for the FA Charity
Shield?
2. What was the ZDS Cup?
3. Vinny Samways' goal won the 1995 Charity Shield for
which team?
4. What 'first' was created by Birmingham City's winning goal
in the Wembley Final of the 1995 Auto Windscreen Shield?
5. Which Italian side defeated Port Vale to lift the 1996 Anglo-
Italian Cup?
6. Prior to 1993, what usually happened when the Charity
Shield match finished level after 90 minutes of play?

Half-Chance

7. What became England's first commercially-sponsored
tournament in 1970?
8. And what was the criterion for entry into that competition?
9. Who scored Everton's winner in the 1987 Charity Shield
match, 15 years after his brother Allan had headed the only
goal of the FA Cup Final?
10. Which club has won the Welsh Cup most often since 1878?
11. Which team set a record score for a Wembley Charity
Shield victory in 1978?

12. Can you name either of the strikers who each scored hat-tricks in the 1989 Simod Cup Final between Everton and Nottingham Forest?

Long-Range Shot
13. In 1981, Scottish clubs ended their involvement in the Anglo-Scottish Cup tournament. What was ironic about the reason they gave for their withdrawal?
14. Which two teams drew 6-6 in a ZDS Cup first round tie in October 1991?
15. What was the Debenhams Cup?
16. Which goalkeeper scored in the 1967 Charity Shield match?
17. Who were the first and only winners of the Scottish Spring Cup in 1976?
18. In May 1988, over 80,000 fans watched which two Fourth Division sides meet at Wembley in the Sherpa Van Trophy Final?

Sharp in the Box
Which team played in four consecutive Charity Shield matches during the 1980s?

QUIZ 8

LEAGUE CHAMPIONSHIP HISTORY

'I came very close to winning a Championship medal with Everton in 1986. While any team can win the Cup, it's invariably the best team that takes the League title.'

Open Goal

1. Which team won the last of the old-style First Division Championships in 1992?

2. How many Championships did Arsenal win under George Graham?

3. Which was the last team to win three consecutive League titles?

4. With which club did Peter Shilton win a Championship medal in 1978?

5. Who was Manchester United manager when the Reds won the 1967 League Championship?

6. Where did Arsenal clinch the 1989 Championship in dramatic style?

Half-Chance

7. Which team won the Championship by a record 13 points margin in 1985?

8. Who was the leading goalscorer for Aston Villa's successful side of 1981?

9. Can you name the Scot who skippered Leeds to the title in 1974?

10. During the 1970s, a team learned that they had won the Championship while on holiday in Majorca. Who were they?

11. Which Lancashire side were First Division Champions in 1960?

12. In which decade did Sunderland last win the League title?

Long-Range Shot

13. Which is the only team to have won the Championship while remaining undefeated?

14. How many times did Bob Paisley manage Liverpool to the title?

15. Who are the only champions to have won the title by winning less than half of their matches?

16. Which club enjoyed a three-in-a-row Championship success from 1924 to 1926?

17. In 1962, which team won the First Division Championship in what was their first-ever season in the top division?

18. Do you know which famous manager guided them to that triumph?

Sharp in the Box

Leeds United finished runners-up in the League Championship on five occasions between 1965 and 1972. Can you name the clubs who pipped them for the title?

Quiz 9

COME ON YOU SPURS

'I had no hesitation when Tottenham came in for me in 1989. They're one of the world's most famous clubs and they play the sort of football I like.'

Open Goal
1. Which European tournament have Spurs won twice?
2. Which former Tottenham star won a European Championship medal in 1996?
3. This defender, who shares a name with the capital city of Scotland, moved to White Hart Lane in 1990. Who is he?
4. Which bird is featured on Spurs' club crest?
5. Who skippered Tottenham to their FA Cup triumphs of 1981 and 1982?
6. Who did Gerry Francis succeed as boss?

Half-Chance
7. In the 1960s, what slight change did Spurs traditionally make to their playing kit in European matches?
8. From which club was Teddy Sheringham signed?
9. Whose superb free-kick strike gave Tottenham a fifth-minute lead in the 1991 FA Cup semi-final against Arsenal at Wembley?
10. Which England manager won a League Championship medal with Spurs in 1951?
11. In which year did goalkeeper Ian Walker make his League debut?
12. The skipper of Spurs' 1961 'Double' team died in December 1993. Can you name him?

Long-Range Shot

13. When did Tottenham last play in the old Second Division?
14. Which team ended Spurs' reign as FA Cup holders by defeating them in the third round of the 1992 competition?
15. Who did Spurs play in the Charity Shield match, the season following their 'Double' victory?
16. Against which team did they enjoy their record European victory, in 1971?
17. Who was the manager of the famous 'push-and-run' side of the late 1940s and early '50s?
18. In which position did Spurs finish in the 1995-96 Premiership table?

Sharp in the Box

Three members of the Tottenham team which won the FA Cup in 1991 had played in the Final with other clubs. Can you name them?

QUIZ 10

MY STRIKING PARTNERS

*'Throughout my career, I was fortunate enough
to play alongside some of the best attackers in
the game. Each had his own special qualities.'*

Open Goal
1. Which Welsh international striker played alongside Gary at Barcelona?
2. With which club has Gordon Durie won three championship medals?
3. Which of Gary's former Leicester team-mates was the old First Division's leading goalscorer in the 1988-89 and 1990-91 seasons?
4. For which country did one-time Everton colleague Graeme Sharp win twelve international caps?
5. Which of Gary's England partners has scored over 200 League goals for Wolves?
6. And which of them played at one time for Canadian side Vancouver Whitecaps?

Half-Chance
7. Who notched a double against both West Germany and the USA during England's summer tour of 1985?
8. Graeme Sharp became player-manager of which First Division club in November 1994?
9. What is Gordon Durie's nickname?

10. Can you name the Portuguese international who starred alongside Gary for the Rest of the World side in the Football League Centenary match staged at Wembley in August 1987?
11. For which Bundesliga club did Mark Hughes play during his spell in European soccer?
12. How many goals did Alan Smith score in the home leg of Arsenal's 1991-92 European Cup tie against Austria Vienna?

Long-Range Shot
13. In which year did Peter Beardsley make his England debut?
14. Can you name the former Partick Thistle striker who scored 21 League goals for Leicester between 1980 and 1982?
15. Everton's Adrian Heath later followed Gary to Spanish football. For which team did he play?
16. Name the former Barcelona striker who had a goal disallowed in the Euro '96 match between Spain and England.
17. Which of Gary's striking partners played for Hibs in the Scottish League Cup Final in 1985?
18. In 1982, Alan Smith won three semi-professional caps for England. Which non-League club was he with at that time?

Sharp in the Box
Peter Beardsley was on the books of five different English clubs between 1979 and 1996. Can you name them?

QUIZ 11

SOCCER IN THE MIDLANDS

*'Being from the Midlands, I like to see the
area's teams do well – especially Leicester,
my home town club.'*

Open Goal
1. Which was the last Midlands club to win the League Championship?
2. Where do Nottingham Forest play their home matches?
3. Which Midlands club were runners-up in the 1996 First Division?
4. Who replaced Barry Fry as Birmingham City manager?
5. In what colour of shirts do Leicester play?
6. Which Midlands club has played in England's top division since 1967?

Half-Chance
7. Which team has won more often in Aston Villa v Birmingham derby matches?
8. Who captained Wolves to three League Championships during the 1950s?
9. Which is the oldest league club in the Midlands and possibly the world?
10. Name the midfielder who followed manager Brian Little from Leicester to Aston Villa in 1995.
11. Which Uruguayan team defeated Nottingham Forest in the World Club Championship match of 1980?

31

12. Which Irish international striker played in Football League Cup Finals for both Leicester and Wolves?

Long-Range Shot
13. Who scored the goal which won the 1995 Auto Windscreen Shield for Birmingham?
14. Which Midlands club did Ian Greaves manage between 1983 and 1989?
15. In both the 1969-70 and 1970-71 seasons, the First Division's leading goalscorer was a West Bromwich Albion player. Can you name the two strikers concerned?
16. Which Midlands team are nicknamed 'The Saddlers'?
17. Who is Leicester's most-capped England international of all time?
18. For which country did Notts County's Rachid Harkouk appear in the 1986 World Cup?

Sharp in the Box
Can you list the five men who have won the PFA Player of the Year award while on the books of a Midlands club?

QUIZ 12

THE CAPTAINS

*'I was absolutely delighted when Graham Taylor
made me captain of England. It was a tremendous
honour to lead the lads out of the tunnel
at Wembley.'*

Open Goal
1. Which country did Danny Blind skipper in Euro '96?
2. Who captained Blackburn to the Premiership title in 1995?
3. Richard Gough replaced Terry Butcher as which club's captain in 1990?
4. Who captained England's World Cup-winning side of 1966?
5. Which star midfielder was dubbed 'Captain Marvel' by Manchester United and England fans?
6. Who has skippered Arsenal to two League Championships since 1989?

Half-Chance
7. Which team did Steve Potts captain in the 1995-96 Premiership?
8. Who led England on eight occasions while a QPR player during the 1970s?
9. Who was the first British club captain to lift the European Cup?
10. Which one-time Wolves skipper later became a player-manager of Rotherham United and a director of Hull City?
11. Martin Buchan is the only man to have captained both Scottish and English FA Cup-winning sides. Which two teams did he lead?

12. Who was the last goalkeeper to skipper a World Cup winning team?

Long-Range Shot
13. What age was Barry Venison when he captained Sunderland in the 1985 Milk Cup Final?
14. Who was the first Liverpool captain to lift the FA Cup?
15. Who is the only man to have been ordered off while captaining England?
16. Who was the then 24-year-old who skippered Crystal Palace in the 1994-95 Premiership?
17. What was the full christian name of famous Sunderland skipper Raich Carter?
18. What distinction does Cuthbert Ottaway hold?

Sharp in the Box
Name the four players called 'Bill' or 'Billy' who have captained post-war FA Cup winning teams.

QUIZ 13

THE PRIDE OF MERSEYSIDE

'Having played there with Everton, I know all about the passion that Merseyside fans have for the game.'

Open Goal

1. Name the Scottish international striker signed by Everton from Rangers in December 1994.
2. Who was Liverpool's top scorer for the second consecutive season in 1995-96?
3. What is Everton's rather 'sweet' nickname?
4. Which Merseyside club plays at Prenton Park, Birkenhead?
5. Which TV analyst captained Liverpool to the League and Cup 'Double' in 1986?
6. Which is the older club – Liverpool or Everton?

Half-Chance

7. Which team ended Everton's reign as FA Cup holders in the 1996 fourth round?
8. From which club did Liverpool sign Jamie Redknapp?
9. This former Everton wing-half masterminded Tranmere's progression from Division Four to Division Two between 1987 and 1991. Who is he?
10. Which team did Liverpool slam ten goals past within the space of ten days in October 1995?
11. What was the result of Joe Royle's first match as Everton manager?

12. Which striker played and scored for both clubs in Merseyside derby matches during the 1970s?

Long-Range Shot
13. Who was the only Liverpool player to appear in all 51 League and cup matches during The Reds' successful 1987-88 season?
14. Which graduate of the FA School of Excellence made his debut for Everton in February 1989?
15. Who made his Scotland debut as a Liverpool player in 1979 but never actually played a first-team match at Anfield?
16. Name the Merseyside rivals who were team-mates in England's World Cup-winning team of 1966.
17. Which team did Everton defeat in the 1989 FA Cup semi-final?
18. The first-ever orderings off in a Merseyside derby match occurred in the Anfield clash of October 1979. Can you name either of the players involved?

Sharp in the Box
Name the six men who managed Everton between 1970 and Joe Royle's appointment as boss in 1994.

QUIZ 14

IRISH CREAM

*'Although it's only in recent years that the
Republic have made an impact in international
soccer, Irish stars have always played a big
part in English League football.'*

Open Goal

1. From which club did Manchester United sign Roy Keane?
2. Which Irish international striker was the English First Division's leading league goalscorer in 1995-96?
3. Who skippered the Republic of Ireland in the 1994 World Cup finals?
4. Which club bought Steve Staunton from Liverpool in 1991?
5. Veteran Irish defender David O'Leary holds the appearance record at which London club?
6. Can you name either of the teams for which Frank Stapleton netted FA Cup Final goals?

Half-Chance

7. Republic of Ireland midfield star Jason McAteer was actually born in which part of England?
8. Which Irishman netted the only goal of the 1991 Rumbelows Cup Final?
9. What was the last English League club for which Liam Brady played?
10. Can you name the London-born QPR and Arsenal defender who won five caps for the Republic during the 1970s?
11. Who replaced Jack Charlton as Ireland manager during 1995-96?

12. Name the Wolves striker who shot Ireland into the lead in the infamous abandoned 'friendly' against England in February 1995.

Long-Range Shot
13. Can you list the three clubs for which Ray Houghton played before joining Liverpool in 1987?
14. In which year did Andy Townsend make his international debut?
15. Who was the Republic's first black international star?
16. With which club did Denis Irwin make his English League debut in 1984?
17. Irish wing star of the 1980s, Tony Galvin, has a degree in which European language?
18. Do you know the name of the Arsenal player who was capped by Ireland at both soccer and rugby during the 1940s?

Sharp in the Box
Name the five other countries in the Republic of Ireland's qualifying group for the 1998 World Cup.

QUIZ 15

THE MEN WHO KEEP THEM OUT

*'For 90 minutes, they're the arch-enemy of
any striker, but I've got great respect for
most goalkeepers.'*

Open Goal
1. Who is England's most-capped goalkeeper of all time?
2. With which club has Tim Flowers won a Premiership medal?
3. Which former Liverpool goalkeeper was involved in allegations of match-fixing during 1994-95?
4. What nationality is Peter Schmeichel?
5. Which Premiership goalkeeper played in both the 1994 World Cup finals and Euro '96?
6. Goalkeeper Jonathan Gould is the son of which well-known manager?

Half-Chance
7. For which team did Scotland goalkeeper Jim Leighton play during 1995-96?
8. Who was the on-loan 'keeper who took Leighton's place in Manchester United's 1990 FA Cup Final team?
9. Shaka Hislop joined Newcastle United from which First Division side in 1995?
10. Which goalkeeper was ordered off during the 1994 World Cup finals?

11. Who kept goal in the League Cup Finals of 1985 and 1991, for Sunderland and Sheffield Wednesday respectively?

12. What was the Scottish connection between the respective goalkeepers in the Republic of Ireland v England match of November 1990?

Long-Range Shot

13. Can you name the three goalkeepers who appeared in the 1982 European Cup Final between Aston Villa and Bayern Munich?

14. What age was Derek Forster when he kept goal for Sunderland against Leicester in a 1964 First Division match?

15. Karol Wojtyla was, at one time, a goalkeeper with a Polish amateur team. How is he better known?

16. Motherwell's 1991 Scottish Cup Final hero joined Rangers the following year. Who is he?

17. Why did Manchester United 'keeper Ray Wood spend much of the 1957 FA Cup Final playing on the right wing?

18. What unusual aid did both Jack Kelsey and Gordon Banks use in their goalkeeping?

Sharp in the Box

Name the four clubs for which David Seaman has played league football.

QUIZ 16

OH GARY, GARY...

'I've quite a few footballing namesakes.
See how much you know about them ...'

Open Goal

1. Which Gary has kept goal for both Manchester United and Middlesbrough?

2. Former England full-back Gary Stevens played in three FA Cup Finals for which Merseyside club during the 1980s?

3. Which Manchester United defender was capped by England while a Second Division player?

4. In which national team would you find Gary Speed?

5. Which Gary missed a penalty during the England-Scotland match during Euro '96?

6. Garry Flitcroft left which club to join Blackburn Rovers in March 1996?

Half-Chance

7. Do you know which Gary scored 18 League goals for Aston Villa's Championship side of 1981?

8. Which important match of Euro '96 did Gary Neville miss through suspension?

9. Which Gary swapped the red of Liverpool for the blue of Everton in January 1992?

10. Can you name the Manchester United and England goalkeeper who was forced to quit top-class football by a bad knee injury?

11. Gary Smith's unfortunate own goal cost his team the 1992 Scottish League Cup Final. Which team was that?

12. From which club did Leeds sign Gary McAllister?

Long-Range Shot
13. Which team did Gary Gillespie captain at the age of 17?
14. Can you name the Republic of Ireland 'B' international goalkeeper who joined Bury from Newcastle in 1989?
15. Who was the first 'Garry' to be transferred for £1 million?
16. At which club did Gary Bowyer play alongside his dad Ian in April 1990?
17. Who was Spurs' substitute in both the 1981 and 1982 FA Cup Finals?
18. Which Gary was joint top scorer in the Endsleigh League Second Division during 1995-96?

Sharp in the Box
Five players with the christian name Gary took part in the 1991 FA Cup Final between Tottenham and Nottingham Forest. How many can you name?

QUIZ 17

EURO '96

'Euro '96 was a great success and it was
good to see England regain their status as a
major force in international football.'

Open Goal

1. Who captained the victorious German team in the Final of Euro '96?
2. What label was given to Oliver Bierhoff's sudden death extra time winner in that match?
3. Which England star was the tournament's top scorer with five goals?
4. Who struck Scotland's only goal of Euro '96?
5. Which team opened the scoring in the Final?
6. Who did England defeat in a penalty shoot-out at the quarter-final stage?

Half-Chance

7. For which country did Joao Pinto and Ricardo Sa Pinto star?
8. Which Scotland midfielder made a goal-line 'save' with his hand during the group match against Holland?
9. Name the Parma-based striker who netted in all of his country's games at Euro '96.
10. True or false: the 31 matches were watched by over one million spectators?
11. Who was on target three times for Croatia during the finals, including a superb chipped goal against Denmark's Peter Schmeichel?

43

12. Which player scored against his own club goalkeeper in a first round match?

Long-Range Shot
13. What was the highest-scoring match of Euro '96?
14. Which country's fans scooped the 'best supporters' award?
15. Name the English referee who yellow-carded ten players during the Germany-Czech Republic group match.
16. Which country fielded a player from the USA's Major League Soccer?
17. Which was the only team to come from behind to win a match?
18. Can you remember the French player who missed a penalty in the semi-final shoot-out?

Sharp in the Box
Name the four quarter-final venues at Euro '96.

QUIZ 18

WORLD CUP '94

*'The 1994 World Cup was probably the best
tournament since 1970. There was lots of
positive football and some really
spectacular goals.'*

Open Goal

1. Brazil won the 1994 World Cup on a penalty shoot-out.
What was the score after 120 minutes of the Final?
2. Who won the Golden Ball award as the Player of the
Tournament?
3. Which Eastern European country ended Germany's reign
as World Champions by defeating them in the quarter-finals?
4. Why was Diego Maradona kicked out of the Finals?
5. Which 1994 World Cup manager was banned from the
touchline in one of his team's first round matches?
6. Was the Final staged in New York or Pasadena?

Half-Chance

7. What was the result of the third place play-off in USA '94?
8. Only two teams breached the Brazil defence during the
tournament – who were they?
9. Which of the competing players designed his own shirts?
10. In which city was the opening match played?
11. Who scored in each of Germany's first four matches of the
finals?
12. What special significance did the timing of the USA v
Brazil second round match have for the American public?

Long-Range Shot

13. Which was the only team to fail to score in the 1994 World Cup finals?

14. In which position did Ireland finish in their first round group?

15. Can you name the Bolivian who was the first player to be red-carded in the tournament?

16. Apart from runners-up Italy, which other two sides were eliminated on penalties?

17. Which of the competing countries had the youngest team?

18. What was the total number of goals scored during the finals – 101, 121 or 141?

Sharp in the Box

Can you name the four qualifying third-placed teams in the 1994 World Cup finals groups?

QUIZ 19

LIONS OF ENGLAND

*'It's a highly illustrious list of names who
have worn the famous white shirt of
England down the years.'*

Open Goal

1. Alan Shearer won his first England cap at which club?
2. Which Spurs striker netted twice in England's Euro '96 match against Holland?
3. In which year's World Cup Finals did Paul Gascoigne firmly establish himself on the international scene?
4. Name the brothers in England's Euro '96 squad.
5. Who did Glenn Hoddle succeed as England boss?
6. Three players appeared for England in each of the 1982, 1986 and 1990 World Cups. Can you name any of them?

Half-Chance

7. Who won the more caps – Des Walker or Kenny Sansom?
8. Which member of England's 1966 World Cup winning team played in contact lenses?
9. Can you name the Southampton forward who was England's top goalscorer in the 1973-74, '75-76 and '76-77 seasons?
10. Name the former Turkish League player who was included in England's Euro '96 squad.
11. Striker Malcolm Macdonald netted five goals against Cyprus in 1975. How many of them were headers?
12. Who was the first man to captain and then manage England?

13. How many caps did Glenn Hoddle win – 43, 53 or 63?

14. Which club provided seven players for the England team which played against Italy in 1934?

15. Can you name the South African-born, Ipswich Town midfield man who was capped twice by England in the 1975 Home International Championship?

16. Which England wing star of the 1940s and '50s was nicknamed 'The Preston Plumber'?

17. With which two clubs was Rodney Marsh capped?

18. Who scored for both sides in England's friendly against Holland in March 1988?

Sharp in the Box
Can you list four men who played for England between 1946 and 1995 and whose surnames contain the letter 'x'?

QUIZ 20

EURO '92

'Denmark's victory in Sweden was a real surprise to everyone. It just underlined how unpredictable football can be.'

Open Goal
1. Which country did the Danes defeat in the Final?
2. Which of the tournament favourites lost on a penalty shoot-out in the semis?
3. Can you name the Swedish marksman who hit three goals in the competition, including the strike which knocked England out?
4. Which city staged the Final?
5. Who netted England's only goal?
6. Which country was expelled from the tournament only eight days before it began?

Half-Chance
7. Which Scotland player scored his first goal in 26 internationals when he was on target in the match against the CIS?
8. How many of their five matches did Denmark actually win?
9. Who was the German captain who broke his arm in his team's opening game?
10. Where did England play their first two matches?
11. Which Scotland player was appearing in the country of his birth?

12. Which national manager complained that his team had only played well for a total of 25 minutes during their three matches?

Long-Range Shot
13. Who played in the right-back position for England against Sweden?
14. How many Rangers players took part in the Scotland-CIS match?
15. Can you name the manager of the triumphant Denmark team?
16. What unusual basis did Scotland use for the numbering of their players?
17. Who was Germany's top scorer in the Finals, with three goals?
18. What nationality was the Final referee Bruno Galler?

Sharp in the Box
Only two of the competing teams in Euro '92 didn't contain any English-based players. Who were they?

QUIZ 21

WORLD CUP '90

*'I think we proved a lot of people wrong when
we reached the semi-finals in Italy. With a bit
of luck, we could've gone all the way.'*

Open Goal
1. Who was the manager of 1990 World Cup winners West Germany?
2. Which country defeated England in the third place play-off match?
3. Can you name the two players sent off in the West Germany v Holland second round game in Milan?
4. Which defender headed England's winner in their group match with Egypt?
5. Scotland crashed to a shock defeat in their opening match. Which Central American side beat them 1-0?
6. Who was the German full-back who notched three goals in the tournament, including the winner in the Final?

Half-Chance
7. Italy's Roberto Baggio scored what was probably the best individual goal of the 1990 finals – against which team?
8. Which Argentinian striking star missed the Final through suspension?
9. Which African country had two players ordered off in the tournament's opening match?
10. Which England forward had a goal disallowed in the first half of the second round meeting with Belgium?
11. Where was the England-West Germany semi-final played?

12. In the Final, which German striker was brought down in the penalty area to win the spot-kick award which decided the match?

Long-Range Shot
13. Which player committed more fouls than any other in Italia '90?
14. Who notched his first-ever international goal in Scotland's 2-1 victory over Sweden in Genoa?
15. Which team had the leakiest defence in the tournament, conceding 11 goals in total?
16. Can you name the Argentinian goalkeeper who broke his leg in the match against the Soviet Union?
17. Which team finished bottom of England's first round group?
18. Name the Real Madrid midfielder who hit four goals in Spain's four matches.

Sharp in the Box
Can you name the four beaten quarter-finalists in Italia '90?

QUIZ 22

BEST OF BRITISH

'For countries so small, the Scots, Welsh and Northern Irish have an impressive record in international competition.'

Open Goal

1. In which year's World Cup Finals did Northern Ireland enjoy a famous victory over hosts Spain?
2. Which Manchester United star became the youngest Welsh cap of all time when he played against Germany in October 1991?
3. What colour of jerseys do Scotland traditionally play in?
4. Name the manager who guided Northern Ireland to two World Cup Final tournaments during the 1980s.
5. For which of the home countries does Vinnie Jones play?
6. In which year did all four home nations reach the World Cup Finals?

Half-Chance

7. Where did Scotland begin their 1998 World Cup qualifying campaign?
8. Which Welsh defender missed a penalty at a crucial stage of his country's 1993 World Cup qualifier against Romania in Cardiff?
9. Can you name the 59-times-capped Northern Ireland international who has managed both Arsenal and Tottenham?
10. In which year's World Cup Finals did Scotland remain undefeated in their three matches?

11. Who is Wales' most-capped player of all time?
12. Whose September 1991 hat-trick against the Faroe Islands saw him equal the Northern Ireland goalscoring record?

Long-Range Shot
13. At which club was Dean Saunders first capped?
14. Who was Scotland's manager at the 1978 World Cup in Argentina?
15. In which year did Wales reach the quarter-Finals of the European Championship?
16. How many Northern Ireland caps did George Best win?
17. Who was the last player to score four goals in one match for Scotland?
18. In November 1983, Northern Ireland became the first team to win a European Championship match on West German soil. Who scored their winning goal in Hamburg?

Sharp in the Box
Can you name the four men who managed Wales between Mike Smith's two spells in charge?

Quiz 23

World Cup '86

*'After a bad start, England really came good
in Mexico. We were disappointed not to progress
further than the quarter-finals.'*

Open Goal

1. Who scored a goal with 'the Hand of God'?
2. Can you name the giant stadium in Mexico City which staged the Final between Argentina and West Germany?
3. England notched their first win of the tournament against which Eastern European country?
4. Which goalkeeper won a world-record 119th cap during the Finals?
5. Two players in the England squad shared the same name. Who were they?
6. Which diminutive midfielder scored Scotland's only goal?

Half-Chance

7. Can you name the two England players who were with a foreign club at that time?
8. The World Cup holders met the European Champions in a second round match. Which teams were involved and who won?
9. Against which country was Ray Wilkins given his marching orders?
10. Nico Claesen, who scored three goals for Belgium in '86, joined which English club later that year?
11. Who kept goal for West Germany in the Final?
12. What was the injury which forced Bryan Robson to bow out of the tournament?

Long-Range Shot

13. Which country notched the biggest win of the 1986 Finals?
14. Tomas Boy skippered which team?
15. What was the name of the official mascot, a smiling, green chilli-pepper?
16. For which country did 'Romerito' net two first-round goals?
17. What dramatic name did the locals give to Scotland's tough first-round group?
18. Who was the only English referee to officiate in the Finals?

Sharp in the Box

Seven Manchester United players travelled to Mexico as members of four World Cup squads. How many of them can you name?

QUIZ 24

WORLD CUP – PAST HISTORY

'Every World Cup tournament has its own particular memories for fans – famous goals, famous saves and even famous tears!'

Open Goal

1. Can you name the only South American country to have won a World Cup tournament which was held in Europe?
2. Which was the last host nation to win the Cup?
3. Who was the Italian striker who top-scored in the 1982 World Cup in Spain?
4. Which team did England defeat in the semi-Finals in 1966?
5. Can you name the Dutch superstar who refused to travel to the 1978 World Cup, much to the disappointment of his countrymen?
6. What was the result of every opening match in the World Cup tournaments between 1966 and 1978 inclusive?

Half-Chance

7. Who skippered Brazil to victory in 1970?
8. Which was the first World Cup Finals tournament to feature 24 teams?
9. Who missed England's final three matches in 1966 after sustaining a four-inch shin gash in the group match against France?
10. Which was the lowest-scoring World Cup tournament in terms of goals-per-game?

11. The player who scored the first goal of the 1974 World Cup Finals also scored the last goal of the 1982 tournament. Can you name him?

12. Who was the first player to score in every round including the Final?

Long-Range Shot

13. In which year did the USA shock England with a 1-0 victory?

14. Which competing country had the biggest travelling support in the 1974 World Cup in West Germany?

15. Who was the Dutchman who wore a plaster cast on his injured arm during the 1978 Final against Argentina?

16. In which year were substitutes first allowed in the tournament?

17. Can you name the two countries who, in 1958, played out the first-ever 0-0 draw in the World Cup Finals?

18. What was the name of England's 1982 mascot?

Sharp in the Box
Name the six European countries which have lost in a World Cup Final.

Quiz 25

The Managers

'I had several managers throughout my career and I think I can safely say that I learned something from all of them.'

Open Goal
1. Who was sacked as Arsenal manager in August 1996?
2. Which team did Joe Royle boss between 1982 and 1994?
3. Which manager is nicknamed 'Harry'?
4. Who did Craig Brown succeed as Scotland manager?
5. Who is the only man to have twice managed English 'Double' winning teams?
6. At the beginning of the 1994-95 season, two former World Cup winners were in charge of Premiership teams. Can you name them?

Half-Chance
7. Which country's manager won the "coaches' coach" award at Euro '96?
8. At which club did Trevor Francis begin his management career?
9. Glaswegian Jimmy Sirrel had three spells in charge of which East Midlands club between 1969 and 1987?
10. In what position did Mike Walker play during his days as a pro?
11. Which manager has enjoyed play-off success with Plymouth, Notts County and Huddersfield?
12. Which Premiership manager reached the top of the German pop charts in 1979?

Long-Range Shot

13. Who managed the Great Britain team in the 1948 Olympic Games football tournament?
14. Who was the first manager to take Brighton into England's top flight?
15. Who was George Graham's last signing as Arsenal manager?
16. Which former Manchester United and Northern Ireland star bossed Raith Rovers to victory in the 1994-95 Scottish First Division and Coca-Cola Cup?
17. Who preceded Jack Charlton as Republic of Ireland boss?
18. In 1966, Ted Bates led which club into Division One for the first time in their history?

Sharp in the Box
Can you name the four English clubs which Graham Taylor has managed?

QUIZ 26

HAVE BOOTS
WILL TRAVEL

*'In football, it's important to make the
right move at the right time.'*

Open Goal
1. From which club did Blackburn sign Chris Sutton?
2. Who became Britain's first £2 million player when he
moved from Newcastle to Spurs in 1988?
3. At which London club did Andy Cole begin his career?
4. Which former Crewe Alexandra player has cost more than
£17 million in transfer fees since 1991?
5. Which member of England's 1966 World Cup team made
over 100 League appearances for each of Blackpool, Everton,
Arsenal and Southampton?
6. Name the international striker who played in the Scottish
Premier League for five different clubs.

Half-Chance
7. Who rejoined Birmingham from Stoke in March 1996?
8. Veteran defender John McClelland has played League
football in all four home countries since 1974. For which
country was he capped 53 times?
9. Can you recognize this player by his transfer trail –
Bournemouth-Chelsea-Liverpool-QPR-Rangers-Chelsea-
Sheffield United?
10. Which two internationals did Leeds sign from Sheffield
Wednesday in the summer of 1994?

11. Charlie George helped Arsenal win the 'Double' in 1971, but at which club did he win his only England cap?

12. Can you name the two clubs for which Steve Bruce played before joining Manchester United?

Long-Range Shot

13. At which club did Graeme Souness begin his professional career?

14. Who, in September 1979, became the first uncapped player to be sold for more than £1 million?

15. For how many different Football League clubs did Leslie Roberts play between 1921 and 1936?

16. Colourful England striker Frank Worthington was a man of many clubs but at which of them did he win a Second Division Championship medal in 1970?

17. Who played in the European Cup competition for three different Scottish clubs?

18. What was Lee Dixon's first club?

Sharp in the Box
Can you name the five British clubs for which Mark Hateley has played up to 1996?

QUIZ 27

THE FOREIGN LEGION

*'English fans seem to enjoy watching the
foreign stars. They add a certain je ne sais quoi!'*

Open Goal

1. With which two clubs has Eric Cantona won English
Championship medals?

2. Which Italian international joined Chelsea from Juventus
in the summer of 1996?

3. Dutchman John de Wolf appropriately joined which
English side in 1994?

4. This 'Great Dane' appeared in three FA Cup Finals between
1986 and 1992. Who is he?

5. From which club did Everton sign Marc Hottiger?

6. What nationality is Uwe Rosler?

Half-Chance

7. Which 1995-96 Premiership captain was born in the USA?

8. Name the Bolton striker who hit all four goals in Finland's
1994 European Championship victory over San Marino.

9. Which English club did Argentinian World Cup star
Alberto Tarantini join in 1978?

10. Which of Spurs' foreign signings scored the winner in the
North London derby of January 1995?

11. Who was the German prisoner-of-war who won an FA
Cup winners medal with Manchester City in 1956, despite
breaking his neck during the Final?

12. Who was the first overseas player to win the Football
Writers' Footballer of the Year award?

Long-Range Shot

13. Pavel Srnicek was formerly a soldier in which country's army?

14. Where did Zimbabwean international Peter Ndlovu notch a hat-trick for Coventry in March 1995?

15. Nestor Lorenzo, who joined Swindon in October 1990, had achieved what rather ignominious distinction three months previously?

16. Who was the Oxford United player who appeared for New Zealand against England in the summer of 1991?

17. Can you name the Dane who became the first overseas player to win a European competition medal with a British club, when he played for Newcastle in the 1969 Fairs Cup Final?

18. Who was the German player, thought to have been the Football League's first foreign import in 1907?

Sharp in the Box

Two members of Liverpool's 1986 'Double' team were born in South Africa. Can you name them?

Quiz 28

Early Exchanges

*'The opening period of many games can be
quite hectic as players seek to establish an
advantage over their opponents.'*

Open Goal
1. Which current manager holds the record for scoring
England's fastest-ever World Cup goal?
2. Against which country did he net it in 1982?
3. International football's quickest goal of all time was scored
after just 8.3 seconds of which country's 1993 match with
England?
4. Who was booked within five seconds of the kick-off in the
1992 FA Cup fifth round tie between Chelsea and Sheffield
United?
5. Which Blackburn striker netted after 13 seconds of Rovers'
April 1995 match at Everton?
6. Bradford Park Avenue's Jim Fryatt claimed a very quick
goal in April 1965. How long after kick-off did he allegedly
score?

Half-Chance
7. Who was the Manchester United and Ireland player
ordered off after only 85 seconds of the First Division match
at Southampton in January 1987?
8. Which Arsenal defender put through his own goal after 16
seconds of the Gunners' match at Sheffield Wednesday in
February 1990?

9. Jackie Milburn was on the scoresheet within 45 seconds of the start of the 1955 FA Cup Final. For which team did he net?

10. Who scored Wembley's quickest-ever goal, for England against Yugoslavia in 1989?

11. Can you name the English referee who awarded Holland a penalty in the first minute of the 1974 World Cup Final?

12. Which country scored the quickest goal of the 1994 World Cup Finals?

Long-Range Shot

13. In which country was Damian Mori playing when he claimed the fastest goal in football history in December 1995?

14. How long was Bologna's Giuseppe Lorenzo on the pitch before he was red-carded in the 1990 Italian League match with Parma?

15. In the 1973 European Cup Final between Ajax and Juventus, who headed the Dutchmen into a fourth-minute lead?

16. Derek Johnstone headed past Jim Cruickshank in the first minute of the 1976 Scottish Cup Final. Which teams were playing?

17. Which England forward was on target within 17 seconds of a 1947 match against Portugal in Lisbon?

18. Hungary trounced England 6–3 at Wembley in 1953. Can you name their deep-lying centre-forward who netted the first of his three goals in the opening minute of the game?

Sharp in the Box

Can you name the four teams which have come from behind to win a World Cup Final?

Quiz 29

You are the Ref

*'I've never really had many problems
with referees. It helps to appreciate that
they don't have an easy job.'*

Open Goal

1. Can a goal be scored directly from a corner-kick?
2. Which particular players are governed by the 'four-step' rule?
3. Can a penalty-taker score from a rebound?
4. How many yards should opposing players usually be from the ball at the taking of a free-kick?
5. Can a player ever be offside in his own half of the pitch?
6. What is the distance of the penalty-spot from the goal-line?

Half-Chance

7. True or false: the maximum amount of injury time that can be added on at the end of each half is ten minutes?
8. How does the referee signal a direct free-kick?
9. What is the maximum weight that the ball can be at the start of a match?
10. Should a player be allowed to wear a wrist-watch while playing?
11. True or false: all players, except the kicker and the goalkeeper, have to be behind the ball at a penalty-kick?
12. Where should a substitute enter the field of play?

Long-Range Shot

13. What should be awarded if a defender inside the penalty-area pushes an opponent who is just outside it?

14. Is it permissible for the goalposts to be painted in red-and-white stripes?

15. Can a defender swap places with the regular goalkeeper at a penalty-kick?

16. If a player shouts 'leave it' to a team-mate, should the referee take any action?

17. What is the maximum length allowed for a football pitch?

18. Which is the only Law of the Game which has no International Board decisions applied to it?

Sharp in the Box

Four penalty offences can be committed with the hand. Can you name them?

Quiz 30

4-3-3

'4-3-3, 4-4-2, 3-5-2 – soccer formations are almost a science in themselves now!'

Open Goal

1. Which striker scored in each of his four Wembley appearances for Manchester United during the 1993-94 season?

2. Which of the Bristol teams suffered three successive relegations between 1980 and 1982?

3. Which famous player appeared in three World Cup-winning teams for Brazil?

4. Which team slammed four goals past Manchester United in a 1994 Champions League match?

5. Can you name the three major trophies won by Liverpool in the 1983-84 season?

6. Three brothers turned out for Southampton against Sheffield Wednesday in October 1988. What was their surname?

Half-Chance

7. Name the Spanish striker who hit four World Cup goals against Denmark in 1986?

8. Between 1974 and 1995, Edinburgh was home to three Scottish League clubs. Which of them relocated in '95?

9. Can you name the three Manchester United players who have been European Footballer of the Year?

10. Which team defeated Liverpool 4-3 in a thrilling FA Cup semi-final in 1990?

11. Which two countries drew all three of their first round matches in the 1982 World Cup?

12. Three German teams have played in the European Cup Final since 1970. Who are they?

Long-Range Shot

13. Which team had four players ordered off during a 1994 Scottish First Division defeat by Airdrie?

14. Three players grabbed hat-tricks in Manchester City's 10-1 thrashing of Huddersfield in November 1987. Can you name them?

15. In which year did the Football League introduce three points for a win?

16. Egyptian international Hossam Hassan fired four UEFA Cup goals against Celtic in 1991. Which team was he on target for?

17. In which year did it take three matches to settle the outcome of the Football League Cup Final?

18. Who was the Real Madrid star of the 1950s and '60s who played at international level for three different countries?

Sharp in the Box
England were the first World Cup-winning team to use a 4-3-3 formation. How many of their 'back four' can you name?

Quiz 31

DRAMATIC DEBUTS

*'I'll always remember my first League
appearance – for Leicester against Oldham
on New Year's Day, 1979.'*

Open Goal

1. Who scored twice on his Blackburn Rovers debut, against Crystal Palace in August 1992?

2. Can you name the Dutch World Cup star who scored in his first Premiership match for Nottingham Forest in August '94?

3. Which international star was ordered off on his Scottish League debut for Rangers against Hibs in 1986?

4. Did Andy Cole score in his first game for Manchester United?

5. Who scored debut goals for each of Chelsea, Spurs, West Ham and England?

6. True or false: in 1977, Celtic's Joe Craig scored for Scotland without having kicked a ball in international football?

Half-Chance

7. How many goals did Len Shackleton bag on his debut for Newcastle against Newport in October 1946?

8. Who scored the first of 30 international goals on his Scotland debut against Wales in Cardiff in 1958?

9. Against which team did Alan Shearer grab a hat-trick on his First Division debut?

10. In May 1984, who launched himself onto the international scene by netting Wales' winner against England in the last Home Championship meeting between the countries?

11. Can you name the goalkeeper, later to play for Watford

and Manchester City, who saved a penalty in the first minute of his Football League debut match, for Birmingham against Sunderland in 1981?

12. In December 1994, former Liverpool star Steve McMahon was ordered off on his debut as player-manager of which club?

Long-Range Shot

13. Where did Ian Wright mark his first appearance for Arsenal with a goal in a Rumbelows Cup tie?

14. How long did it take Barry Jones to score his first goal in Notts County colours in March 1967?

15. Can you name the former Dundee and St Johnstone striker who scored on his Premier League debut for Aberdeen in August 1994?

16. Who was the West Ham striker who scored on his first and only appearance for England, against Iceland in 1982?

17. Against which team did David Platt score in his first Italian League game for Bari in September 1991?

18. Who was the last player to make a scoring debut for England in a World Cup Finals match?

Sharp in the Box

On the opening day of the 1991-92 season, three players scored on their League debut for Aston Villa at Sheffield Wednesday. How many of them can you name?

QUIZ 32

SUPER SUBS

*'I was never on the bench very often but I
did make my England debut as a sub for
Tony Woodcock against Scotland in 1984.'*

Open Goal
1. Name the Israeli international who hit a sensational hat-trick after coming on as a sub during the 1995 Southampton v Spurs FA Cup fifth round replay.
2. The 1989 FA Cup Final saw four of the five goals scored by substitutes. Who netted twice for Liverpool?
3. And who equalized twice for Everton?
4. Who was the 42-year-old substitute who came off the bench to score Cameroon's consolation goal in their 1994 World Cup match against Russia?
5. For which team did Ian Wright score two FA Cup Final goals as a substitute in 1990?
6. What unusual substitution was made during the 1994 World Cup tie between Mexico and Bulgaria?

Half-Chance
7. Who netted four goals in five appearances as substitute for Manchester United during 1990?
8. For which team was Ray Kennedy a scoring sub in the 1970 Fairs Cup Final first leg against Anderlecht?
9. In which year's World Cup Final did a substitute score a goal before being replaced himself?
10. Who was Liverpool's 'supersub' of the 1970s who later played for Lucerne, Wigan, Oldham, Beveren and Tranmere?

11. Eddie Kelly was the first No. 12 to score in an FA Cup Final, but who originally claimed the goal which Kelly scored?

12. Who booked his country's place in the 1974 World Cup Finals by heading a decisive goal against Czechoslovakia after he had replaced Kenny Dalglish?

Long-Range Shot

13. Who was Spurs' match-winning sub in the 1973 League Cup Final against Norwich?

14. Paul Gascoigne scored his first England goal as a substitute in the Wembley World Cup match against which country in April 1989?

15. Who was the first substitute to score in a World Cup Final?

16. Can you name the sub who headed Aberdeen's dramatic late winner in the 1983 European Cup-Winners' Cup Final?

17. Who is the Northern Ireland international goalkeeper who scored for Hull during 1994-95 after taking the field as a substitute striker?

18. Lazlo Kiss came off the bench to grab a hat-trick in a 1982 World Cup Finals match. For which country was he playing?

Sharp in the Box

In which year did the Football League first permit a) one substitute per team and b) two substitutes per team in League matches?

QUIZ 33

QUITE A SEASON – 1995-96

'There was some classic action served up in 1995-96. For example, the Liverpool-Newcastle match at Anfield was an absolute cracker.'

Open Goal

1. Who hit a hat-trick against Aberdeen to clinch the Scottish League Championship for Rangers?
2. Which Premiership goalkeeper headed an equalizer during a UEFA Cup match in September 1995?
3. What was the Bosman Ruling?
4. Against which team did Eric Cantona score on his long-awaited comeback in October?
5. Which London-based Premiership club contemplated a move to Dublin?
6. At which ground did Holland defeat the Republic of Ireland to qualify for the 1996 European Championship Finals?

Half-Chance

7. Which visiting goalkeeper thrilled Wembley with a spectacular scorpion-kick save in September 1995?
8. Which was the first team to be eliminated from the 1995-96 Champions League?
9. Who won the African Nations Cup on home soil?
10. Which veteran English League striker received an MBE in the 1996 New Year honours list?

11. Who moved from Galatasaray to Southampton in October?

12. Who scored his 100th League goal for Newcastle United during the '95-96 season?

Long-Range Shot
13. Which team inflicted Ajax's first defeat in 53 games, in January 1996?

14. Who won the 1996 Vauxhall Conference?

15. Which two players launched the 'International Association of Professional Footballers' in September '95?

16. Which Second Division side shocked Manchester United by winning 3-0 at Old Trafford in the Coca-Cola Cup?

17. Can you name the 1996 football film which starred Sean Bean as Sheffield United hopeful Jimmy Muir?

18. Why was the Brighton v York match abandoned after 13 minutes?

Sharp in the Box
England defeated three European countries in Wembley friendlies during 1995-96. Can you name them?

Quiz 34

ROUND THE GROUNDS

*'I must have played in over 100 different football
stadia. My favourite English League ground
is Everton's Goodison Park.'*

Open Goal

1. Where do Chelsea play?
2. Maine Road is home to which club?
3. What is Scotland's national football stadium called?
4. This club made an emotional return to their ground The
Valley in December 1992. Who are they?
5. Which stadium is sometimes called 'The Venue of
Legends'?
6. True or false: Manchester United's Old Trafford ground is
used for Test cricket during the summer months?

Half-Chance

7. Which Scottish League club's ground is in England?
8. Plough Lane is the former home of which English
Premiership club?
9. Where do Ipswich Town play?
10. In which town is Grimsby's Blundell Park actually
situated?
11. Can you name the stadium which made World Cup history
by staging the 1994 USA v Switzerland Finals match indoors?
12. On the opening day of the 1986-87 season, the Victoria
Ground, Hartlepool staged two Football League matches.
Apart from the local side, who else played 'at home' that day
and why?

Long-Range Shot

13. Which ground holds the record for the highest attendance in the old Fourth Division and also for the lowest crowd ever recorded at a top division match in England?

14. In 1938, British Prime Minister Chamberlain met Adolf Hitler at a place called Oberwiesenfeld. Which famous stadium is now situated on that site?

15. What have Ninian Park, Dean Court and McDiarmid Park in common?

16. The Boleyn Ground is the official name of which club's home ground?

17. Who plays at Springfield Park?

18. Name the new stadium to which Northampton Town moved in 1994.

Sharp in the Box
Name the three Scottish grounds in which European competition finals have been played.

Quiz 35

Quite a Season – 1994-95

'Although footballers were often in the news for the wrong reasons, 1994-95 was still a memorable season for the English game.'

Open Goal

1. Which Manchester United midfielder scored with an overhead kick in the Charity Shield match with Blackburn?
2. Who broke John Radford's record of 11 goals in European competition for Arsenal?
3. Who scored twice for England against the USA in September?
4. Which trophy did Celtic win?
5. Which former England manager led FC Porto to their 13th League Championship success?
6. Who spoke about 'seagulls, trawlers and sardines' in March?

Half-Chance

7. Which former Soviet republic trounced Wales 5-0 in a European Championship match?
8. Who scored his first goal for England in the friendly against Romania?
9. Which award did Robbie Fowler receive from the PFA in April?
10. What was the aggregate score in the European Super Cup match between AC Milan and Arsenal?

11. How did Kenny Dalglish emulate Brian Clough and Herbert Chapman in 1995?

12. Can you remember the name of the Turkish team which knocked Aston Villa out of the UEFA Cup?

Long-Range Shot

13. Which team did Birmingham City put seven goals past on New Year's Eve?

14. Who was ordered off in the North London derby of January 1995?

15. Which Arsenal striker scored the first Premiership goal of the season?

16. Which Premiership star made a speech to the Oxford University student union in May?

17. Which team won the first-ever Scottish Third Division championship?

18. Why were Exeter City not demoted to the Vauxhall Conference despite finishing bottom of Division Three?

Sharp in the Box
Can you name the four forward players who appeared as substitutes in the 1995 FA Cup Final?

QUIZ 36

ON THE SPOT

'The penalty-kick has been with us for over 100 years but, with so many cup ties being decided by shoot-outs these days, it's more important than ever.'

Open Goal

1. Which England defender missed his penalty in the Euro '96 semi-final shoot-out with Germany?
2. Where should a goalkeeper be at the taking of a penalty-kick?
3. Who missed the first penalty of the 1994 World Cup Finals – in the opening ceremony?
4. Where did David Seaman save three penalties during a 1995 European semi-final shoot-out?
5. Raith Rovers lifted the 1994 Scottish Coca-Cola Cup after a shoot-out blunder by which Celtic and Scotland star?
6. Name either of the England players who missed kicks in the 1990 World Cup semi-final shoot-out against West Germany.

Half-Chance

7. Who had his penalty saved during the Italy-Germany group match of Euro '96?
8. Which was the first team to win an FA Cup semi-final on a shoot-out?
9. How many spot-kicks were Inter Milan awarded in their Italian League match against Verona in September 1991?
10. Which Premiership side did Wolves knock out of the 1995 FA Cup on penalties?

11. Who put Manchester City ahead in the 1981 FA Cup Final replay by firing home a second-half penalty?

12. Can you remember which goalkeeper saved a penalty during the 1988 Littlewoods Cup Final between Arsenal and Luton?

Long-Range Shot

13. Fifteen penalty-kicks were awarded during the 1994 World Cup Finals – how many were scored?

14. What delayed the taking of Gerry Daly's penalty for Derby in the match against Manchester City in April 1977?

15. Who was the Dutchman who hit four penalty goals during the 1978 World Cup Finals?

16. Can you name Spurs' goalkeeping hero of the 1984 UEFA Cup Final penalty shoot-out?

17. Peter Shilton only saved one penalty during his 125-game international career. Do you know who the penalty-taker was?

18. In November 1988, Argentinos Juniors eventually defeated Racing Club in the longest penalty shoot-out on record. What was the final result?

Sharp in the Box
Name the five England players who converted their kicks in the Euro '96 semi-final shoot-out.

Quiz 37

QUITE A SEASON –
1993-94

*'England's World Cup elimination was an obvious
disappointment but '93-94 was an enjoyable season,
especially if you were a Manchester United fan!'*

Open Goal
1. Who hit 41 League and Cup goals for Newcastle United?
2. And which Englishman was the Scottish Premier League's
leading scorer?
3. Who broke his right leg during a training session in Rome?
4. Which team were barred by UEFA from defending the
European Cup?
5. Can you name the former Manchester City star who
became the Maine Road club's new chairman in February
1994?
6. For how many matches was John Toshack in charge of
Wales?

Half-Chance
7. What ignominious century did Swindon chalk up in 1993-
94?
8. Who were England's representatives in the Final of the
Anglo-Italian Cup?
9. Which Endsleigh League side lost in a penalty shoot-out in
the 1994 Coca-Cola Cup semi-finals?
10. Which two Italian sides did Arsenal defeat in lifting the
European Cup-Winners' Cup?

11. Which Scandinavian country provided the opposition for Terry Venables' first match as England boss?

12. Who was the Football Writers' Footballer of the Year for 1993-94?

Long-Range Shot

13. What was unusual about the crowd at the Rangers-Celtic match of April 1994?

14. Can you name the former Arsenal and Ipswich star who guided Hibernians to the Maltese Championship?

15. Why was the April 1994 Germany v England friendly international called off?

16. Which country won the African Nations Cup?

17. Who escaped FA disciplinary action after writing graffiti on West Ham's dressing-room wall?

18. Which city hosted the draw for the 1996 European Championship qualifying competition?

Sharp in the Box
Can you remember which two Chelsea players conceded penalties in the 1994 FA Cup Final?

Quiz 38

Record Breakers

*'Although not all players might admit it, breaking
a record does give a lot of satisfaction.'*

Open Goal
1. Who bagged a Premiership record five goals for
Manchester United against Ipswich in March 1995?
2. Who, in November 1983, became the first player to net 100
League goals for a single club in both Scotland and England?
3. Which club smashed the British transfer record for a
defender when they bought Des Walker from Sampdoria in
July 1993?
4. Who is the youngest player ever to have appeared in the
World Cup Finals?
5. Which team has won the FA Cup on a record nine occasions?
6. Can you name the Italian goalkeeper who set a new
international clean-sheet record during the 1990 World Cup?

Half-Chance
7. Which was the only club to have played in the Premier
League plus all six previous divisions of the old Football
League?
8. Can you name the Birmingham City striker who, at 6' 7",
was the Endsleigh League's tallest player in 1995-96?
9. Who is the only man to have been both England and
Scotland's Footballer of the Year?
10. In 1958, France's Just Fontaine set a new record for the
most goals in a single World Cup tournament. How many
did he score?

11. Which goalkeeper became the first British player to appear in 1,000 first-class matches when he played for Arsenal against West Bromwich in February 1983?

12. Which team had the lowest points total in British senior football in 1995-96?

Long-Range Shot

13. Who scored a British record 37 hat-tricks during his career at Tranmere, Everton and Notts County?

14. Rangers set a new Scottish Premier Division goals-for record in 1991-92. Did they score 81, 91 or 101?

15. What is thought to be the oldest international fixture in continental Europe?

16. Which team set an unenviable new record for successive penalty misses in September 1991?

17. Which ground holds the attendance record for a League match in England?

18. Who is reputedly the world's leading goalscorer of the post-war era?

Sharp in the Box

Can you name the players who broke the £1,000, £10,000 and £100,000 British transfer records respectively?

QUIZ 39

QUITE A SEASON – 1992-93

'FIFA's new back-pass rule was the big innovation of 1992-93. I think the fans enjoy the drama which it can sometimes create.'

Open Goal

1. Which two British sides clashed in the European Cup second round during '92-93?
2. Who retired after 18 years as manager of Nottingham Forest?
3. Both FA Cup semi-finals in 1993 featured derby matches. Can you name the teams involved?
4. Who was fined £20,000 for his part in the video *Soccer's Hard Men*?
5. Karren Brady became the new managing director of which club?
6. In December 1992, who became only the second modern-day player to score for both clubs in Merseyside derby games?

Half-Chance

7. How many of their away League matches did champions Leeds win in 1992-93?
8. Who resigned as Crystal Palace manager in May?
9. Where did Ian Wright score his first goal for England?
10. Which Republic of Ireland star went AWOL before a World Cup qualifying match?
11. Who hit a club record 42 League goals for Portsmouth?

12. Where did Ally McCoist break his leg while playing for Scotland?

Long-Range Shot
13. Which club won the inaugural Konica League of Wales?
14. Can you name the Olympic sprinter who had a week's trial with Wigan in March 1993?
15. Which country notched their first-ever World Cup point after drawing 0-0 with Turkey?
16. Why was the Leeds-Stuttgart European Cup tie replayed?
17. Who netted two Premier League hat-tricks in the space of three days over the Easter holiday period?
18. How many Liverpool players were red-carded during the season?

Sharp in the Box
The 1993 FA Cup Final ended in a draw, but which player picked up a medal that day and why?

QUIZ 40

SOCCER – THE WORLD GAME

'The advance which football has made in places like Japan and the USA really just confirms its position as the world's most popular sport.'

Open Goal
1. What is the name of Japan's First Division?
2. Which African country lost practically its entire national squad in a 1993 air crash?
3. USA international Cobi Jones signed for which English Midlands team in 1994?
4. Which prestigious international club match has been staged in Tokyo since 1980?
5. Can you remember which Asian country shocked Italy with a 1-0 victory in the 1966 World Cup?
6. Name the World Cup legend who became Brazil's Minister of Sport in 1995.

Half-Chance
7. What is South America's equivalent of the European Championship called?
8. In which country does a team called Barcelona play at the Monumental?
9. Where was the first-ever Women's World Cup held in 1991?
10. In which year did New Zealand reach the World Cup Finals?
11. Can you name the Argentinian side which defeated AC Milan in the 1994 World Club Championship match?

12. In which Japanese city could you watch the Flugels play the Marinos?

Long-Range Shot
13. The highest-ever official attendance at a club match was recorded at a 1963 derby game in Rio de Janeiro. 177,656 watched which two teams in opposition?
14. In which country does the team Hearts of Oak play?
15. Which country hosted the World Youth Cup in 1995?
16. Can you give the name of Morocco's leading army side?
17. Which country became a footballing El Dorado in the 1950s, after forming a pirate league outwith the jurisdiction of FIFA?
18. Who was the former Blackpool and England goalkeeper who, as national coach of Canada, took that country to their first-ever World Cup Finals in 1986?

Sharp in the Box
Who were Asia's two representatives in the 1994 World Cup Finals?

QUIZ 41

THE CHAMPIONS' CUP

*'Despite tentative beginnings in the 1950s,
the Champions' Cup is now clearly the ultimate
prize in European club football.'*

Open Goal

1. Which was the first English team to win the European Cup?
2. Where was the 1996 Champions' Cup Final held?
3. Ronald Koeman has won European Cup medals with two clubs. Can you name them?
4. Who was the last Englishman to play in a European Cup Final?
5. Which Greek side knocked Rangers out of the 1994-95 tournament?
6. In which city have Liverpool twice won the Cup?

Half-Chance

7. Can you name the French international who took part in the three European Cup Finals from 1993 to 1995?
8. Which was the last Final in which both teams scored?
9. Can you name the Yugoslavian coach and professor of modern history who steered Sampdoria to the 1992 Final?
10. Which team has lost more European Cup Finals than any other side?
11. Who headed Nottingham Forest's winning goal in the 1979 Final against Malmo?
12. Which is the only team to have won the European Cup after a replay?

Long-Range Shot

13. Name the teenager who hit the winning goal of the 1995 Final.

14. Who, in 1991, became the first man to win a European Cup medal with two different clubs?

15. Can you name the manager who led Feyenoord, FC Bruges and SV Hamburg to European Cup Finals between 1970 and 1983?

16. Which team failed to qualify for the 1995 quarter-finals despite taking the lead in five of their six Champions League matches?

17. Which was the first team to win a European Cup tie on the toss of a coin?

18. Who once scored three goals in a European Cup Final but still finished on the losing side?

Sharp in the Box

Can you name the five teams which have won the European Cup at Wembley Stadium?

Quiz 42

Futbol Español

'My three years at Barcelona were a tremendous experience. The fans there were great to me.'

Open Goal

1. Which team won the Spanish 'Double' in 1996?
2. Name the Dutch coach who led Barcelona to four European tournament Finals between 1989 and 1994.
3. Which Spanish side shocked Arsenal in the 1995 Cup-Winners' Cup Final?
4. In which colour shirt does the national team play?
5. Which former Cardiff City and Liverpool star has managed Real Madrid, Real Sociedad and Deportivo La Coruna?
6. What is the name of Barcelona's magnificent home stadium?

Half-Chance

7. Which Romanian World Cup star has played for both Real Madrid and Barcelona?
8. Who were the Canary Islands' representatives in the 1995-96 Spanish First Division?
9. For which Spanish club did John Aldridge play?
10. Name the goalkeeper who is Spain's most-capped player of all time.
11. What was the former name of Real Madrid's Bernabeu Stadium?
12. Which team lost the 1994 Spanish Championship when they missed a last-minute penalty in their final League match of the season?

Long-Range Shot

13. For which team did Russian international star Victor Onopko play during 1995-96?

14. Which Spanish club reached three consecutive Fairs Cup Finals during the 1960s?

15. Can you name the Atletico Madrid goalkeeper who set a new world shut-out record of 1,275 minutes in March 1991?

16. Which city is home to Real Betis?

17. Who was the last Spaniard to be voted European Footballer of the Year?

18. To whom is the *Pichichi* trophy awarded each year?

Sharp in the Box

Between 1980 and 1992, German international Bernd Schuster played for three top Spanish clubs. Name them, in the order in which he joined them.

QUIZ 43

STARS OF EUROPE

*'I've played with and against most of Europe's
top stars of recent years. For me though,
Michel Platini, with his delicate through passes,
was simply a striker's dream.'*

Open Goal

1. Name the German international who has won
Championship medals with both Bayern Munich and Inter
Milan.

2. For which team did twin brothers Frank and Ronald de
Boer star in 1995-96?

3. Who became the most expensive Bulgarian footballer of all
time in 1990?

4. Vitor Baia keeps goal for which country?

5. Who is the classy sweeper who skippered AC Milan to
European Cup success in 1989 and 1990?

6. In which year did Michel Platini lead France to victory in
the European Championship?

Half-Chance

7. Who was the goalkeeper selected for FIFA's 1994 World
Cup team of the tournament?

8. Holland's Dennis Bergkamp is reputedly named after
which famous British international striker?

9. Can you name the Hamburg-based player whose goal
knocked Germany out of the 1994 World Cup?

10. Patrik Berger is an international star for which country?

11. Name the AC Milan defender who missed both the

European Cup Final and World Cup Final in 1994 after being yellow-carded in the respective semi-finals.

12. Which much-capped Belgian full-back captained PSV Eindhoven to an impressive 'Treble' of League, Cup and European Cup in 1988?

Long-Range Shot

13. Can you name Switzerland's most-capped player of all time?

14. With which club did Franz Beckenbauer win a German *Bundesliga* Championship medal in 1982?

15. In which part of the former Yugoslavia was Dejan Savicevic born?

16. Brian and Michael Laudrup are the sons of a former Danish international star. What is his name?

17. During the 1970s, who succeeded Johan Cruyff as captain of both Ajax and Holland?

18. Polish international Krzysztof Warzycha scored the winning penalty in which country's 1995 Cup Final?

Sharp in the Box
Four Germans were voted European Footballer of the Year between 1970 and 1991. How many of them can you name?

THE CUP-WINNERS' CUP

*'I was fortunate enough to win a medal in this
competition with Barça in 1989. We beat
Sampdoria 2-0 in the Final in Berne.'*

Open Goal

1. A goal from which former Spurs star won the 1995 Cup-Winners' Cup for Real Zaragoza?
2. Where was the 1996 Final played?
3. Which manager has led two different British clubs to Cup-Winners' Cup success?
4. Who hit both of Manchester United's goals in the 1991 Final against Barcelona?
5. Which team did Marco van Basten captain in the '87 Final?
6. Who scored twice when Sampdoria defeated Anderlecht to win the trophy in 1990?

Half-Chance

7. Which was the last German side to lift the Cup-Winners' Cup?
8. Where did Rangers defeat Moscow Dynamo in the 1972 Final?
9. Can you name the New Zealand international striker who was on the scoresheet in the 1992 Final?
10. Which team knocked Everton out of the 1995-96 tournament?
11. Which club reached three consecutive Cup-Winners' Cup Finals during the 1970s?

12. Manchester United's run as Cup-Winners' Cup holders ended when they lost to which Spanish team in the 1991-92 second round?

Long-Range Shot
13. Who were England's first representatives in the European Cup-Winners' Cup?
14. Can you name the Georgian team which Celtic defeated home and away during the 1995-96 competition?
15. How many different Liverpool players scored in the home leg of the Reds' 1974 Cup-Winners' Cup tie against Stromsgodset of Norway?
16. Which club won the Cup-Winners' Cup at Wembley in 1965?
17. Which was the last club to win the tournament who were not the holders of their own national cup?
18. In the first round of the 1991-92 tournament, Swansea incurred the heaviest defeat ever sustained by a senior Welsh club in European competition. What was the aggregate score of their tie against Monaco?

Sharp in the Box
A Scotsman, an Englishman and an Irishman were all on the scoresheet in Everton's 1985 Cup-Winners' Cup Final victory over Rapid Vienna. Can you name the players concerned?

QUIZ 45

CALCIO – THE ITALIAN LEAGUE

*'Although I never played club football in
Italy, I do rate their football highly – there
are so many quality players.'*

Open Goal

1. Which team is known as *'La Vecchia Signora'* (The Old Lady)
of Italian football?
2. Which club did Paul Ince join in the summer of 1995?
3. In which city do Lazio play?
4. What are the colours of Fiorentina?
5. Where is the stadium known as San Siro?
6. For years in Italy, there has been dispute over the number of
stranieri which should be allowed in each team. What are they?

Half-Chance

7. Who was the first American international to play in the
Serie A?
8. Who competes for the Italian Super Cup?
9. Who finished 1995-96 as the *Serie A*'s joint-top goalscorer,
despite having played in a relegated side?
10. What impressive new record did AC Milan set while
winning the Italian Championship in 1991-92?
11. Which veteran *Serie A* defender is nicknamed 'The Tsar'
because of his Russian ancestry?
12. Who was coach at Inter Milan when they last won the
championship?

Long-Range Shot

13. Which was the last Sardinian club to win the Italian title?

14. Who were the two Englishmen signed by Bari for £800,000 in June 1985?

15. Which club lost its *Serie A* place after losing a relegation play-off to Padova in June 1995?

16. Talented midfield star Gianni Rivera was which club's most popular player during the 1960s and '70s?

17. How many different clubs have won the Italian 'Double'?

18. What was unusual about Michaelangelo Rampulla's headed equalizer for Cremonese against Atalanta in February 1992?

Sharp in the Box

Name the six Italian clubs which have played in the European Cup Final since 1956.

THE UEFA CUP

*'In some ways, the UEFA Cup can be the hardest
of all the European tournaments. There are more
rounds to play and so many strong teams.'*

Open Goal

1. Who won the 1996 UEFA Cup?
2, Which English team reached the quarter-finals in '95-96?
3. In what way has the UEFA Cup Final traditionally differed from the European Cup and Cup-Winners' Cup Finals?
4. Can you name the two English clubs which won the competition during the 1980s?
5. Which is the only Scots club to have played in the Final – Aberdeen or Dundee United?
6. Name the French team which lost in the '96 Final.

Half-Chance

7. Who hit five goals for Juventus against CSKA Sofia in a 1994-95 second round second leg match?
8. Which was the last part-time club to win the tournament?
9. Who was Liverpool's manager when the Reds first won the UEFA Cup?
10. Which Danish side shocked Real Madrid with a last-minute winner in a third round tie in December 1994?
11. Jurgen Klinsmann won a UEFA Cup runners-up medal with which club in 1989?
12. Which Scot scored 14 goals in the 1980-81 tournament?

Long-Range Shot

13. What was the full original title of the competition which eventually became the UEFA Cup?

14. Who scored both home and away when Norwich defeated Bayern Munich in 1993-94?

15. With which club did South Korea's Cha Bum-Kun win a UEFA Cup medal in 1988?

16. Do you know the name of the Englishman who scored for Finnish side Kuusysi Lahti against Liverpool in the 1991-92 competition?

17. Which was the last team to win the UEFA Cup in successive seasons?

18. In the 1970-71 Fairs Cup tournament, a team played out twelve matches undefeated yet still failed to lift the trophy. Who were they?

Sharp in the Box
Four clubs have won all three major European club trophies. Can you name them?

Quiz 47

THE FRENCH CONNECTION

'France has produced some very talented footballers despite, in my opinion, having a relatively weak domestic league.'

Open Goal

1. Which French team lost in the 1996 European Cup semi-finals?
2. What is the chief venue used by the national team for their home matches?
3. Who was stripped of the captaincy of France in January 1995?
4. Which club is known as *l'OM*?
5. Which European club tournament did Paris Saint-Germain win in 1996?
6. Can you name the French international defender who has played for Marseille, Rangers and Monaco?

Half-Chance

7. Which team won the League and Cup 'Double' in France in 1996?
8. Who are known as *'Les Verts'* (The Greens)?
9. What is the meaning of Marseille's club motto *'droit au but'*?
10. Can you name the Corsican team which played in the 1995 French League Cup Final?
11. In which year did Glenn Hoddle and Mark Hateley win a French League Championship medal with Monaco?

12. Which French side did Manchester United defeat in the quarter-finals of the 1991 European Cup-Winners' Cup?

Long-Range Shot
13. Who was the Belgian who coached Marseille to victory over Milan in the 1993 European Cup Final?
14. Basile Boli's elder brother has been a prolific goalscorer in French soccer for more than a decade. What is his name?
15. For which club have Britons Eric Black and David Hodgson played?
16. Known as 'Manu', this son of a Spanish immigrant won championship medals with both Monaco and Marseille. Who is he?
17. How did Valenciennes defender Jacques Glassmann shock French football in May 1993?
18. In which French First Division stadium is there a spectators' car park underneath the pitch?

Sharp in the Box
Three French teams have played in the European Cup Final. Can you name them?

Quiz 48

CONTINENTAL HIT-MEN

*'It's a tough job scoring goals in Europe's
top leagues. You have to admire the men
who do it regularly.'*

Open Goal

1. Which sportswear company traditionally awards a 'Golden Boot' to Europe's leading league goalscorer?
2. Name the Liberian-born striker who moved from Paris Saint-Germain to Milan in the summer of 1995.
3. What was the nickname of the 1970s German goal-getter Gerd Muller?
4. In which national side would you find strikers Stephane Chapuisat and Kubilay Turkyilmaz?
5. Which top French marksman has the initials JPP?
6. With which club did both Rudi Voller and Alen Boksic both win a European Champions' Cup medal?

Half-Chance

7. Dennis Bergkamp's goals helped which team to European trophy success in 1992?
8. Which club was Hristo Stoichkov playing for when he won the 1990 Golden Boot award?
9. Who was the Russian striker who hit a record five goals in the 1994 World Cup Finals match against Cameroon?
10. From which club did Real Madrid sign Croatian hot-shot Davor Suker?

11. Can you name the now-retired FC Bruges striker who hit 23 goals in a record 96 appearances for the Belgian national team?

12. Who is the Swedish international hit-man who won two national championships in the calendar year 1994, with Ajax and IFK Gothenburg?

Long-Range Shot

13. Two strikers scored hat-tricks in the 1994-95 UEFA Cup first round, first leg tie between Bayer Leverkusen and PSV Eindhoven. Name either.

14. Eusebio is the Portuguese national side's all-time top goalscorer, but in which country was he born?

15. Which French-based player notched five goals in the 1994 World Cup Finals?

16. This Austrian international has played for Austria Vienna, Torino, Ascoli, Seville, Logrones and Cologne. Who is he?

17. Which Turkish former Golden Boot winner caused a sensation in the summer of 1991 when he left Istanbul's Galatasaray for their deadly local rivals Fenerbahce?

18. Why was Dynamo Dresden's 1991 East German Footballer of the Year, Torsten Gutschow, at the centre of a political controversy in January 1992?

Sharp in the Box

Rangers' Ally McCoist was Europe's top league goalscorer in 1992 and 1993. Name the three other Scots who also finished in the top three of the Euro scoring charts between 1968 and 1983.

Quiz 49

Sporting Soccer Fans

*'Like many other sportsmen, my good friend
snooker star Willie Thorne is a football nut.'*

Open Goal
1. Name the top sports promoter who became the new
chairman of Leyton Orient in April 1995.
2. Which former Wimbledon tennis champion congratulated
his fellow Germans as they lifted the Henri Delaunay trophy
at Euro '96?
3. This Dundee United fan has been women's 10,000 metre
world champion. Who is she?
4. Which famous golfer was at Wembley to cheer on
Barcelona in the 1992 European Cup Final?
5. Which former British 1,500 metre athlete is a big fan of
Sunderland?
6. Hearts can include the six-times world snooker champion
among their supporters. Who is he?

Half-Chance
7. Which is the favourite football team of swimmer Zara Long
and tennis commentator Gerry Williams?
8. Which former England cricket captain is an admirer of
West Ham?
9. Which club does athletics commentator David Moorcroft
follow?
10. What is the favourite team of cue star Steve Davis?

11. Snooker's Jimmy White, cricketer Alec Stewart and darts star Eric Bristow are all fans of which team?

12. Can you name the BBC racing commentator who has been a keen follower of Swindon Town for many years?

Long-Range Shot

13. Which is the favourite football team of former British tennis star John Lloyd?

14. This Chelsea supporter has played both Rugby Union and Rugby League for Wales. Who is he?

15. Boxer Pat Clinton used the facilities of his favourite football club to train for his world flyweight title fights. Which club was this?

16. Can you name the former Great Britain Rugby League scrum-half who travelled to Istanbul to watch Manchester United play Galatasaray in September 1994?

17. Former Wimbledon champion Stefan Edberg claims to be a supporter of which English team?

18. Channel Four's extrovert racing pundit follows Newcastle United. Who is he?

Sharp in the Box

England Under-21 international Ian Brightwell is the son of two former British Olympic athletes. Can you name them?

QUIZ 50

READ ALL ABOUT IT

'I can hardly keep up with all the soccer books and magazines on the market now – the fans certainly can't complain about a shortage of reading material.'

Open Goal

1. Which is Britain's oldest weekly soccer magazine?
2. Name Nick Hornby's classic football book.
3. Supporters of which club produce the fanzines *An Imperfect Match* and *The Gooner*?
4. In which country is there a football magazine called *Kicker*?
5. Who wrote the book entitled *It's a Funny Old Life*?
6. Which particular type of players are the subject of Bob Wilson's book *You've Got To Be Crazy*?

Half-Chance

7. In which comic does the football character 'Billy the Fish' appear?
8. What is reputedly Britain's biggest-selling football club newspaper?
9. Can you name the writer, a connoisseur of Italian football, who joined *The People* in 1992 after 33 years with *The Sunday Times*?
10. Who is the subject of the book *Mr Smith*?
11. Which former England manager's autobiography is entitled *Against The Odds*?
12. In which country could you buy the daily football and sports paper called *Marca*?

Long-Range Shot
13. To what does the book *The Glory, Glory Nights* refer?
14. Name the FA coach who wrote the book *The Winning Formula*.
15. Which club is the subject of Jeff Kent's *The Valiant Years*?
16. Who is featured in the book *Green Gunners*?
17. What is the name of the Milan-based daily sports paper founded in 1896?
18. What witty title did Stuart Cosgrove give to his book on scandal in Scottish football?

Sharp in the Box
What is the derivation of the St Johnstone fanzine title *Wendy Who?*

QUIZ 51

HOWZAT!
FOOTBALLING
CRICKETERS

*'I showed a lot of promise as a cricketer at school
but, in the end, I had to decide to concentrate
on my football.'*

Open Goal

1. Which West Indian cricket star played for Antigua in the
qualifying tournament for the 1978 soccer World Cup?

2. Which Scottish international goalkeeper has represented
his country in the NatWest trophy?

3. For which English League club did Ian Botham play?

4. Which member of England's 1966 World Cup-winning
team was also an occasional first-class cricketer with Essex?

5. Which Steve played for Arsenal, Brighton and Charlton
and is the brother of a famous cricketer?

6. Which Test cricket ground staged the first ever FA Cup
Final in 1872?

Half-Chance

7. Which distinguished Test batsman won an FA Cup winners
medal with Arsenal in 1950?

8. Who kept goal for Aston Villa's 1975 League Cup-winning
side, the year after he had helped Worcester take the County
Championship?

9. Which former England cricket captain first played League football for Bradford City in 1952?

10. He won a League Championship medal with Arsenal and later managed Chelsea to the title. He also played county cricket for Hampshire – who is he?

11. Which ground staged Test and county cricket until 1973 before the resident football club built a new stand on top of the cricket pitch?

12. Which of Manchester United's Neville brothers was once offered terms by Lancashire CCC?

Long-Range Shot

13. England cricket manager Mickey Stewart turned professional with which soccer club in 1956?

14. Who skippered both Lincoln City and Worcester CCC during 1982-83?

15. Which Rangers manager of the 1950s and '60s was capped five times by the Scotland cricket team?

16. Who played Fourth Division football (for Doncaster Rovers) and County Championship cricket (for Leicestershire) on the same day in September 1975?

17. Can you name Woking's FA Cup hero of January 1991 who has represented Gibraltar at cricket?

18. The Glasgow ground of West of Scotland CC staged the first-ever Scotland-England soccer international in 1872. Can you name it?

Sharp in the Box
Football borrowed the expression 'hat-trick' from cricket. Do you know the origin of the term?

Quiz 52

The Colours

*'Strips change a lot more often than they used to.
For instance, I must have worn about four different
designs of England jersey during my career.'*

Open Goal
1. In what colour jerseys did England win the World Cup in
1966?
2. What are the colours of West Ham?
3. Which English Premiership side play in blue-and-white
halved jerseys?
4. What colour was the controversial away strip ditched by
Manchester United in 1996?
5. What is the distinctive feature of the Ajax Amsterdam jersey?
6. Can you name the two Scottish Premier League sides who
play in green and white?

Half-Chance
7. Which leading English side introduced numbered stocking
tabs during the early 1970s?
8. How did Liverpool's Robbie Fowler beat the FA's 1995 ban
on players removing their shirts when celebrating a goal?
9. Which sportswear firm supplies both England and
Scotland's kit?
10. Describe the unusual jersey worn by the Croatian national
team.
11. In August 1991, which First Division club's new away
jersey was likened to a 'bruised banana'?
12. What are Darlington's colours?

Long-Range Shot

13. Which current Premiership side wore an unusual chocolate-coloured away kit in the early 1980s?

14. How many official shirt sponsors did Paris Saint-Germain have during 1994-95?

15. In 1961, which Scottish Second Division club changed their colours to yellow and red, partly because their old blue and white strip looked 'too much like Rangers'?

16. Why was Sampdoria's match at Lazio in May 1992 a 'game of two halves' as far as their kit was concerned?

17. What are the colours of *Bundesliga* team Borussia Monchengladbach?

18. George Graham tried to stop Arsenal's players doing it after their 1991 European Cup tie against Austria Vienna and Alf Ramsey stopped the England team doing it with the Argentinians in 1966 – what?

Sharp in the Box
Since 1970, the England national side has played in five different colours of jerseys. What are they?

QUIZ 53

YOU MUST BE JOKING!

*'Every dressing-room has its fair share of jokers.
At Spurs, there was never a dull moment with
the likes of Gazza about.'*

Open Goal

1. Who came up with the legendary quote: 'Football's not a matter of life and death – it's more important than that'?
2. Which much-maligned midfielder said: 'The last time anyone said "good pass" was when I handed over my UB40 to the lady at the dole office!'?
3. Who said in 1994: 'If they sing "Turnip, Turnip, give us a wave", I'll give them a wave'?
4. What happened after Paul Gascoigne jokingly showed the referee a yellow card during the December 1995 Rangers v Hibs match?
5. What was the background to the 1993 headline: 'MAJOR MINOR'S A MINI VINNIE'?
6. Which TV star talked philosophically about supporting Birmingham when he said: 'You lose some, you draw some'?

Half-Chance

7. During the 1991-92 season, which comedian and Liverpool fan joked: 'Any more knocks and we'll be sponsored by BUPA next year!'?
8. Who did journalist Brian Glanville describe thus in 1985: 'He looks corpulent enough to be playing darts for Denmark'?
9. Who complained, after an energetic World Cup qualifying

match for the Republic of Ireland: 'Much more of this and our legs will be worn down to stumps!'?

10. Which stadium did *Guardian* writer David Lacey describe in 1987 as 'The only ground that looks the same in black and white as it does in colour.'?

11. Who was Kevin Keegan talking about when he said after Newcastle's April 1996 victory over QPR: 'I particularly liked their young midfielder'?

12. Which Republic of Ireland defender said in 1990: 'When Ruud Gullit pulls on my shirt at home he'll wonder who the hell's it is'?

Long-Range Shot

13. Which realist of a manager said in 1991: 'Every club I've been at, the chairman gives me £50,000 and says "go on a spending spree"!'?

14. What were West Brom's John Trewick's observations on the Great Wall of China, during Albion's 1978 tour of that country?

15. Who said, on hearing that Charlie Nicholas was leaving Arsenal in 1988: 'Stringfellows will miss him!'?

16. Why did Stoke City striker John Ritchie voice his opposition to Sunday football in 1974?

17. Which BBC commentator came up with this classic: 'For the benefit of those watching in black and white, Spurs are in the yellow shirts!'?

18. Which manager moaned: 'Nowadays, goalkeepers are a more protected species that the Golden Eagle'?

Sharp in the Box

Which controversial ex-manager joked: 'I've had more clubs than Jack Nicklaus' and 'I've been in more courts than Bjorn Borg'?

Quiz 54

The Song Remains The Same

*'I'm always amazed at the repertoire of songs
that the supporters have. It gives players a lift
to hear their name being sung.'*

Open Goal

1. Which Gerry and the Pacemakers' hit was first adopted by Liverpool's Kop choir during the 1960s?
2. Name the two comedians who made the chart-topping 'Three Lions' record with England's Euro '96 squad.
3. Can you remember which opera star had a hit with the 1990 World Cup theme tune 'Nessun Dorma'?
4. What is the Victorian hymn traditionally sung by the Wembley crowd before the FA Cup Final?
5. 'I'm Forever Blowing Bubbles' is the anthem of which club's fans?
6. Who sang a solo part in 'Ossie's Dream' in 1981?

Half-Chance

7. What's the next line of Leeds' 1972 record which begins: 'We play all the way for Leeds United ...'?
8. Which club's fans sing the Pompey Chimes?
9. Can you name the Sandpipers' 1966 hit which has become a popular tune for football fans wishing to highlight the uniqueness of a particular player?
10. What was the title of the official 1994 World Cup theme tune?

11. Who had a 1991 hit with the football fans' favourite 'Always Look on the Bright Side of Life'?

12. Name the old song which has become the adopted anthem of Bristol Rovers supporters.

Long-Range Shot

13. What was the title of the Sunderland fans' 1996 version of the old Monkees hit 'Daydream Believer'?

14. Which team do Oasis stars Liam and Noel Gallagher follow?

15. Which Glasgow club's song begins: 'Hail, Hail …'?

16. Why is 'Simply Red' an appropriate title for singer Mick Hucknall's band?

17. Which Des O'Connor hit did Liverpool's Kop unkindly sing to Leeds goalkeeper Gary Sprake after he had thrown the ball into his own net?

18. Who is the Scotland penalty-taker referred to in the lyrics of their 1982 World Cup record 'We Have a Dream'?

Sharp in the Box

In 1982, who appeared on Top of the Pops with both the Spurs' FA Cup Final team and the Scotland World Cup squad?

SOCCER ON THE BOX

*'The increase in 'live' matches and the advent
of satellite TV have meant a real bonanza
for armchair fans.'*

Open Goal
1. Which BBC highlights programme was first broadcast in 1964?
2. Which former West Ham and England midfielder often co-commentates on England matches alongside John Motson?
3. Who was the manager featured in the 1994 *Cutting Edge* documentary *An Impossible Job*?
4. With which club did ITV presenter Bob Wilson win League Championship and FA Cup medals?
5. Which former TV commentator's most famous line is 'They think it's all over ... it is now!'?
6. Which of the TV companies covered Blackburn and Rangers in the 1995-96 Champions League?

Half-Chance
7. Can you name the Sky Sports commentator who once played for Corinthian Casuals?
8. Which current Premiership boss was seen in TV adverts for *Brut* men's cosmetics during the 1980s?
9. By what nickname is Eurosport commentator Angus Loughran probably better known on television?
10. John Barnes took charge of one of the teams in *A Question of Sport* during 1992. Which footballer did he replace as captain?

11. Who commentated on the 1994 World Cup Final for BBC?

12. TV commentator Alan Parry is a director of which League club?

Long-Range Shot

13. In which year were the World Cup Finals first shown 'live' on British television?

14. Can you name the former *Brookside* actor who presented the fanzine-style football programme *Standing Room Only*?

15. Which non-League side does John Motson follow?

16. Name the BBC Scotland commentator who played in three successive Cambridge v Oxford university matches during the 1960s.

17. Which former Liverpool and Republic of Ireland striker went on to become a football presenter on Spanish television?

18. Which member of the England management team was seen and heard 'rapping' on television during the 1994 World Cup Finals?

Sharp in the Box

Can you name the seven English and Scottish league clubs for which Sky Sports' resident pundit Andy Gray played?

Quiz 56

STRANGE BUT TRUE?

*'Soccer certainly throws up some oddities from
time to time. See if you can separate the fact
from the fiction...'*

Open Goal
1. True or false: Allan Hansen was Europe's fourth highest
goalscorer in the 1981-82 season?
2. Which Liverpool megastar of the 1970s and '80s failed to
impress the club during a trial for their 'B' team against
Southport in 1966?
3. True or false: a Swedish-born player has captained teams in
both the Scottish and English FA Cup Finals since 1987?
4. What is the totally inappropriate middle name of
Liverpool's 1991 signing Mark Walters?
5. True or false: Crewe take the 'Alexandra' part of their name
from Princess Alexandra?
6. Who used his psychic powers to help both Reading and
England during 1996?

Half-Chance
7. Which England international striker allegedly made 34
transfer requests during his time at QPR?
8. How could a team lose a match in the 1945-46 FA Cup, yet
still progress in the tournament?
9. What was strange about Torino's 'away goals' victory over
Juventus in the 1993 Italian Cup semi-final?
10. Which country failed to get a single shot at England's goal
during a 1971 European Championship match at Wembley?

11. Manchester United's European Cup Final goalkeeper once dislocated his jaw while shouting at his defenders. Who is he?

12. Can you name the former Sunderland striker who was the Liberal Democrats' candidate for Sunderland North in the 1992 General Election?

Long-Range Shot

13. How many players called Jones were on Charlton's books in the 1966-67 season?

14. Why were Liberia's players pleased with their goalless draw against Gambia in 1980?

15. Which Scottish League team are nicknamed 'The Blue Brazil'?

16. Which club sacked their PA announcer for criticizing the referee of their 1995 First Division match with Bolton?

17. Why do Moscow Dynamo play in blue and white strips?

18. What ended the football career of Brentford goalkeeper Chic Brodie in 1970?

Sharp in the Box

In every season between 1985 and 1988, the Footballer of the Year was on the losing side in the FA Cup Final. Gary was one (in 1986), can you name the other three?

GO FOR THE CENTURY

*'Here's a hot hundred quick-fire questions to
finish with. See how many you can answer.'*

1. From which club did Newcastle sign Warren Barton?

2. Who are Liverpool's shirt sponsors?

3. What was Alan Ball's first managerial post?

4. Can you name the summer competition which provides
back-door qualification for the UEFA Cup?

5. Which Premiership star received a one-year suspended
sentence for the possession of firearms in September 1995?

6. What is Des Lynam's favourite team?

7. David Ginola won a League Championship medal with
which club in 1994?

8. Which was the last team to retain the FA Cup?

9. At which club did Lee Sharpe begin his League career?

10. Which 62-times-capped England international is a former
sausage factory worker?

11. Who plays at Turf Moor?

12. Name the former Northern Ireland international who has managed Wycombe Wanderers, Norwich and Leicester.

13. Which England international is cousin to boxer Nigel Benn?

14. Which is the only club with an ever-present record in European competition?

15. Can you name the Nottingham Forest defender who won his first England cap in the 1995 Umbro Cup match against Sweden?

16. At which club did Julian Dicks begin his League career?

17. How many Italian League Championship medals did Ruud Gullit win?

18. Who did Ron Atkinson appoint as his assistant manager at Coventry City?

19. Which team does actor Sean Bean follow passionately?

20. Can you name Glenn Hoddle's footballing brother?

21. Which manager signed Jamie Redknapp for Liverpool?

22. Who won the 1996 FA Trophy?

23. Which BBC commentator is a qualified dentist?

24. In which year will the first World Cup of the 21st century be held?

25. Billy Kirkwood replaced Ivan Golac as boss of which club during 1995?

26. What connects Northampton Town with the TV show *Take Your Pick*?

27. Which team did Robbie Fowler and Steve McManaman support as youngsters?

28. From which club did West Ham sign Florin Raducioiu?

29. Who was 'monster shocked, monster stunned' in March 1995?

30. Can you name BBC Scotland's leading female football reporter?

31. How many countries competed in the Finals of Euro '96?

32. Who teamed up with pop group Lindisfarne to record 'Fog on the Tyne' in 1990?

33. In April 1996, which player was re-united with the ball with which he scored a famous hat-trick nearly 30 years previously?

34. Which Scottish League club still uses amateur players?

35. What is Peter Beagrie's favourite goal celebration routine?

36. Which country won the 1995 Copa America?

37. What was Tim Sherwood's first club?

38. How much did Chelsea pay Manchester United for Mark Hughes?

39. 'Harry the Haddock' is the mascot of which club?

40. Which crucial Football League matches were held at Wembley for the first time in May 1990?

41. Why was Fernando Redondo dropped from the Argentinian national side in September 1995?

42. Which country are the reigning women's world champions?

43. Which club has been managed by Gerry Francis, Alan Ball and Terry Cooper?

44. Did Phillipe Albert score for Belgium in the 1994 World Cup Finals?

45. Can you name the two Liverpool team-mates who had a scuffle in a 1993 Merseyside derby match?

46. Which shirt number did Andy Cole take when he joined Manchester United?

47. Graeme Souness coached which Turkish club in 1995-96?

48. Which Midlands team does TV comedian Frank Skinner support?

49. Who replaced Bruce Rioch as Bolton manager?

50. For which Scottish League club did Alan Hansen play?

51. What kind of business does Jurgen Klinsmann's family run?

52. Who was Manchester United's top scorer in season 1995-96?

53. Who were the 'Sky Strikers'?

54. Inside which Premiership ground would you find a bust of legendary manager Herbert Chapman?

55. Can you name the former Hereford and Coventry goalkeeper who went on to become a prophet?

56. Who was re-united with his former manager Frank Clark when he joined Nottingham Forest in the summer of 1995?

57. Which club has had the most recipients of the Football Writers' Footballer of the Year award?

58. What was Terry Venables' nickname at Barcelona?

59. Name the Rangers midfielder who played on loan for Everton during the 1994-95 season before returning to Ibrox.

60. Who did Bryan Robson succeed as Middlesbrough manager?

61. Can you name the Dutch international who played with Dennis Bergkamp at Inter Milan?

62. Which country topped England's qualifying group for the 1994 World Cup tournament?

63. Goalkeeper Mark Bosnich is an international cap for which country?

64. What colour of shirt did referees normally wear in the first four seasons of the Premiership?

65. Which ground staged the 1995 England v Sweden Umbro Cup match?

66. Who was the First Division player-manager who scored a hat-trick at Villa Park in September 1989?

67. At which ground is the Billy Wright Stand?

68. Who was manager of Leeds United prior to Howard Wilkinson?

69. What is Sheffield Wednesday's nickname?

70. Who are Blackpool's closest neighbours in the Nationwide League?

71. Before Aston Villa in '96, which was the last team to win a League Cup Final by a three-goal margin?

72. Which London club's ground is situated in South Africa Road?

73. Who were the 1996 champions of Germany?

74. Nicky Summerbee's dad also played for Manchester City. Can you name him?

75. True or false: Jimmy Hill once ran the line in a First Division match?

76. Name the former Everton star who became Mansfield Town boss in November 1993.

77. Which South American national side plays in white shirts with a red diagonal stripe?

78. Which teams contested the 1996 Charity Shield match?

79. From which club did Coventry sign Eoin Jess?

80. Who scored a hat-trick in the 1996 Scottish Cup Final?

81. Which team do the 'Toon Army' follow?

82. In which year did Peter Shilton make his first-team debut for Leicester City?

83. Don Goodman was which club's top scorer in 1995-96?

84. Despite being born in Preston, Mark Lawrenson was an international cap for which country?

85. Who made German transfer history when he moved from Bayer Uerdingen to Bayern Munich for £2 million in 1990?

86. Which club were once known as Newton Heath?

87. Which country tried to poach Matt Le Tissier before he made his England debut?

88. What was the subject of the Taylor Report which was published in January 1990?

89. Which two national teams at Euro '96 were captained by AC Milan players?

90. What was Colin Hendry's first club?

91. What part does Douglas Fir play at most football matches?

92. How much did Middlesbrough pay Juventus for Fabrizio Ravanelli?

93. Can you name Eric Cantona's younger brother?

94. Gresty Road is home to which Nationwide League club?

95. What is the unusual nickname of Brazilian star Edmundo?

96. Who hit a hat-trick for Leeds in their 1995 UEFA Cup tie in Monaco?

97. Which two countries went to war after a World Cup qualifying match in 1969?

98. Who were the first sponsors of the Football League?

99. This former Premiership and French Second Division striker was born in Scorer Street, Lincoln. Who is he?

100. How many teams play in the Scilly Isles' League?

ANSWERS

QUIZ 1
THE PREMIERSHIP

1. Newcastle United
2. Stan Collymore
3. Ipswich
4. Alan Shearer
5. Spurs
6. Southampton's

7. Liverpool
8. Five
9. Nottingham Forest
10. Aston Villa
11. Middlesbrough's Riverside Stadium
12. Glenn Hoddle

13. Bolton
14. Rick Parry
15. Peter Shilton
16. Steve McManaman
17. Brian Deane
18. 988

Sharp in the Box
Robbie Fowler, Alan Shearer and Tony Yeboah

QUIZ 2
UPS AND DOWNS

1. Leicester City
2. Millwall
3. Peter Reid
4. Three
5. Coventry and Southampton
6. False, they went down in 1974

7. Wimbledon
8. Blackburn
9. Oldham
10. Plymouth
11. Lincoln City
12. Lou Macari

13. Hull
14. 1973-74
15. 'Test Matches'
16. Preston North End
17. Simon Garner
18. They had been champions in the previous season

Sharp in the Box
Spurs (1951), Ipswich (1962) and Nottingham Forest (1978)

QUIZ 3
THE FA CUP

1. The second half
2. Ian Rush
3. Crystal Palace and Manchester United, in 1990
4. Dave Beasant
5. Aston Villa and Chelsea
6. Arsenal, in 1993

7. Terry Venables
8. Sheffield United
9. Norman Whiteside
10. Paul Bracewell
11. Manchester United
12. One (John Aldridge v Everton in 1989)

13. 8-4 to Walsall
14. Brighton
15. Dermott Gallagher
16. Bob Stokoe and Don Revie
17. Leicester (1961), Sunderland (1973) and Crystal Palace (1990)
18. Willie Young

Sharp in the Box
Matt Busby, Tommy Docherty, Dave Sexton,
Ron Atkinson and Alex Ferguson

Quiz 4
To Hull And Back

1. Preston
2. Blackpool
3. Denis Law
4. Scunthorpe
5. Jimmy Hill
6. Wrexham

7. John Chiedozie
8. Doncaster Rovers
9. Aldershot
10. After the crooked spire near their ground
11. The team which has scored the more goals is placed higher
12. Tony Cascarino

13. Darlington
14. Dario Gradi
15. Hereford United
16. Hull
17. Stockport County
18. Headington United

Sharp in the Box
Blackburn, Bristol Rovers, Doncaster, Tranmere,
Albion and Raith

QUIZ 5
SCOTTISH FOOTBALL

1. Ally McCoist
2. Hearts
3. Motherwell
4. Raith Rovers
5. Tangerine and black
6. Partick Thistle

7. Willie Miller
8. Rangers
9. Stirling Albion
10. 40
11. St Mirren
12. Paul and Willie McStay (Celtic, 1985)

13. Kilmarnock
14. Alexei Mikhailichenko and Oleg Kuznetsov
15. Hibs
16. Sandy Jardine
17. Aberdeen
18. Steve Archibald

Sharp in the Box
Celtic, Clyde, Clydebank and Cowdenbeath

QUIZ 6
THE FOOTBALL LEAGUE CUP

1. 3-0
2. Arsenal, in 1993
3. Ron Atkinson
4. Steve McManaman
5. Nottingham Forest
6. Ian Rush

7. David Ginola
8. Wolves
9. John Harkes
10. Old Trafford
11. Clive Allen
12. Arsenal and Birmingham City

13. Alan Hardaker
14. Rochdale
15. Tommy Docherty
16. Birmingham City
17. Morrow broke his arm after being dropped by team-mate Tony Adams during post-match celebrations
18. The Hatters had already been knocked out!

Sharp in the Box
Norwich (1962), QPR (1967), Swindon (1969), Aston Villa (1975) and Sheffield Wednesday (1991)

QUIZ 7
OTHER TOURNAMENTS

1. The League champions and the FA Cup winners
2. The Zenith Data Systems Cup
3. Everton
4. It was the first time a senior Wembley final had been decided by sudden death extra time
5. Genoa
6. Each team retained the trophy for six months

7. The Watney Cup
8. It was open to the two highest-scoring sides in each division (apart from those competing in Europe or achieving promotion)
9. Wayne Clarke
10. Wrexham
11. Nottingham Forest (who beat Ipswich 5-0)
12. Lee Chapman and Tony Cottee

13. They complained that the competing English teams were not strong enough, despite the fact that only one Scottish side had ever won it!
14. Tranmere and Newcastle
15. A once-played two-legged competition for the two lower division clubs which progressed furthest in the FA Cup (Chester beat Port Vale in the one and only Final in 1977)
16. Pat Jennings
17. Airdrie
18. Burnley and Wolves

Sharp in the Box
Everton

QUIZ 8
LEAGUE CHAMPIONSHIP HISTORY

1. Leeds United
2. Two
3. Liverpool
4. Nottingham Forest
5. Matt Busby
6. Anfield, Liverpool

7. Everton
8. Peter Withe
9. Billy Bremner
10. Derby County
11. Burnley
12. The 1930s

13. Preston North End
14. Six
15. Chelsea, in 1955
16. Huddersfield Town
17. Ipswich Town
18. Alf Ramsey

Sharp in the Box
Manchester United, Liverpool, Everton, Arsenal and Derby

QUIZ 9
COME ON YOU SPURS

1. The UEFA Cup
2. Jurgen Klinsmann
3. Justin Edinburgh
4. A cockerel
5. Steve Perryman
6. Ossie Ardiles

7. They replaced their navy shorts and socks with an all-white strip
8. Nottingham Forest
9. Paul Gascoigne's
10. Alf Ramsey
11. 1991
12. Danny Blanchflower

13. 1977-78
14. Aston Villa
15. An FA XI
16. Keflavik
17. Arthur Rowe
18. Seventh

Sharp in the Box
Paul Allen (West Ham), Gary Lineker and Pat van den Hauwe (both Everton)

QUIZ 10
MY STRIKING PARTNERS

1. Mark Hughes
2. Rangers
3. Alan Smith
4. Scotland
5. Steve Bull
6. Peter Beardsley

7. Kerry Dixon
8. Oldham Athletic
9. 'Jukebox'
10. Paulo Futre
11. Bayern Munich
12. Four

13. 1986
14. Jim Melrose
15. Espanol
16. Julio Salinas
17. Gordon Durie
18. Alvechurch

Sharp in the Box
**Carlisle, Manchester United, Newcastle,
Liverpool and Everton**

QUIZ 11
SOCCER IN THE MIDLANDS

1. Aston Villa
2. The City Ground
3. Derby County
4. Trevor Francis
5. Blue
6. Coventry City

7. Aston Villa
8. Billy Wright
9. Notts County
10. Mark Draper
11. Nacional
12. Derek Dougan

13. Paul Tait
14. Mansfield Town
15. Jeff Astle and Tony Brown
16. Walsall
17. Gordon Banks
18. Algeria

Sharp in the Box

Colin Todd (Derby), Andy Gray (Aston Villa), Peter Shilton (Nottingham Forest), David Platt (Aston Villa) and Paul McGrath (Aston Villa)

Quiz 12
The Captains

1. Holland
2. Tim Sherwood
3. Rangers
4. Bobby Moore
5. Bryan Robson
6. Tony Adams

7. West Ham
8. Gerry Francis
9. Billy McNeill (Celtic)
10. Emlyn Hughes
11. Aberdeen and Manchester United
12. Dino Zoff (Italy)

13. 20
14. Ron Yeats
15. Ray Wilkins (who had taken over from the injured Bryan Robson during the 1986 World Cup)
16. Gareth Southgate
17. Horatio
18. He was England's first-ever international captain

Sharp in the Box
Billy Wright, Bill Slater, Billy Bremner and Billy Bonds

QUIZ 13
THE PRIDE OF MERSEYSIDE

1. Duncan Ferguson
2. Robbie Fowler
3. 'The Toffees'
4. Tranmere Rovers
5. Alan Hansen
6. Everton

7. Port Vale
8. Bournemouth
9. John King
10. Manchester City
11. Everton beat Liverpool 2-0
12. David Johnson

13. Steve Nicol
14. John Ebbrell
15. Frank McGarvey
16. Ray Wilson (Everton) and Roger Hunt (Liverpool)
17. Norwich
18. Terry McDermott (Liverpool) and Gary Stanley (Everton)

Sharp in the Box
Harry Catterick, Billy Bingham, Gordon Lee, Howard
Kendall, Colin Harvey and Mike Walker

Quiz 14
Irish Cream

1 Nottingham Forest
2. John Aldridge
3. Andy Townsend
4. Aston Villa
5. Arsenal
6. Arsenal and Manchester United

7. Merseyside
8. John Sheridan
9. West Ham
10. Terry Mancini
11. Mick McCarthy
12. David Kelly

13. West Ham, Fulham and Oxford United
14. 1989
15. Chris Hughton
16. Leeds
17. Russian
18. Dr. Kevin O'Flanagan

Sharp in the Box
Romania, Lithuania, Iceland, Macedonia and Liechtenstein

QUIZ 15
THE MEN WHO KEEP THEM OUT

1. Peter Shilton
2. Blackburn Rovers
3. Bruce Grobbelaar
4. Danish
5. Dmitri Kharine
6. Bobby Gould

7. Hibs
8. Les Sealey
9. Reading
10. Gianluca Pagliuca
11. Chris Turner
12. They both played for Glasgow's Old Firm rivals –
Ireland's Bonner for Celtic and England's Woods for Rangers

13. Spink, Rimmer (Villa) and Muller (Bayern)
14. 15
15. As Pope John Paul II
16. Ally Maxwell
17. He was concussed and unable to take his place in goal
18. They put chewing gum on their hands to improve their
grip

Sharp in the Box
Peterborough, Birmingham City, QPR and Arsenal.

QUIZ 16
OH GARY, GARY...

1. Gary Walsh
2. Everton
3. Gary Pallister
4. Wales
5. Gary McAllister
6. Manchester City

7. Gary Shaw
8. The semi-final against Germany
9. Gary Ablett
10. Gary Bailey
11. Aberdeen
12. Leicester City

13. Falkirk
14. Gary Kelly
15. Garry Birtles
16. Hereford United
17. Gary Brooke
18. Gary Martindale

Sharp in the Box
Gary Lineker and Gary Mabbutt (Spurs), Gary Charles,
Gary Crosby and Garry Parker (Forest)

QUIZ 17
EURO '96

1. Jurgen Klinsmann
2. The 'Golden Goal'
3. Alan Shearer
4. Ally McCoist
5. The Czech Republic
6. Spain

7. Portugal
8. John Collins
9. Hristo Stoichkov
10. True
11. Davor Suker
12. Paul Gascoigne

13. Czech Republic 3 Russia 3, in Group C
14. Holland
15. David Elleray
16. Italy (Roberto Donadoni)
17. Germany
18. Reynald Pedros

Sharp in the Box
Wembley, Old Trafford, Anfield and Villa Park

Quiz 18
World Cup '94

1. 0-0
2. Romario
3. Bulgaria
4. For failing a drugs test
5. Jack Charlton
6. Pasadena

7. Sweden 4 Bulgaria 0
8. Holland and Sweden
9. Mexican goalkeeper Jorge Campos
10. Chicago
11. Jurgen Klinsmann
12. It was played on Independence Day

13. Greece
14. Second
15. Marco Etcheverry
16. Mexico and Romania
17. Saudi Arabia (average age 24 years)
18. 141

Sharp in the Box
USA, Argentina, Italy and Belgium

QUIZ 19
LIONS OF ENGLAND

1. Southampton
2. Teddy Sheringham
3. 1990
4. Gary and Phil Neville
5. Terry Venables
6. Terry Butcher, Bryan Robson and Peter Shilton

7. Kenny Sansom
8. Nobby Stiles
9. Mick Channon
10. Les Ferdinand
11. Four
12. Alf Ramsey

13. 53
14. Arsenal
15. Colin Viljoen
16. Tom Finney
17. QPR and Manchester City
18. Tony Adams

Sharp in the Box
Kerry Dixon, Lee Dixon, Mike Duxbury, Graeme Le Saux,
Albert Quixall and Graham Rix

151

QUIZ 20
EURO '92

1. Germany
2. Holland
3. Tomas Brolin
4. Gothenburg
5. David Platt
6. Yugoslavia

7. Brian McClair
8. Two
9. Rudi Voller
10. Malmo
11. Richard Gough
12. Michel Platini (France)

13. David Batty
14. Seven
15. Richard Moller-Nielsen
16. Apart from the goalkeeper, the players were numbered in an order of seniority based on the amount of caps won
17. Karlheinz Riedle
18. Swiss

Sharp in the Box
Holland and Germany

QUIZ 21
WORLD CUP '90

1. Franz Beckenbauer
2. Italy
3. Frank Rijkaard and Rudi Voller
4. Mark Wright
5. Costa Rica
6. Andy Brehme

7. Czechoslovakia
8. Claudio Caniggia
9. Cameroon
10. John Barnes
11. Turin
12. Rudi Voller

13. Mick McCarthy
14. Stuart McCall
15. The United Arab Emirates
16. Nery Pumpido
17. Egypt
18. Michel

Sharp in the Box
Cameroon, Czechoslovakia, the Republic of Ireland
and Yugoslavia

Quiz 22
Best of British

1. 1982
2. Ryan Giggs
3. Navy blue
4. Billy Bingham
5. Wales
6. 1958

7. Austria
8. Paul Bodin
9. Terry Neill
10. 1974
11. Neville Southall
12. Colin Clarke's

13. Brighton
14. Ally MacLeod
15. 1976
16. 37
17. Colin Stein
18. Norman Whiteside

Sharp in the Box
**Mike England, David Williams (caretaker),
Terry Yorath and John Toshack**

Quiz 23
World Cup '86

1. Diego Maradona
2. The Azteca
3. Poland
4. Pat Jennings
5. Gary Stevens (of Everton and Spurs respectively)
6. Gordon Strachan

7. Mark Hateley and Ray Wilkins
8. Italy v France; France won 2-0
9. Morocco
10. Spurs
11. Toni Schumacher
12. A dislocated shoulder

13. The Soviet Union, who beat Hungary 6-0
14. Mexico
15. 'Pique'
16. Paraguay
17. 'The Group of Death'
18. George Courtney

Sharp in the Box

Gary Bailey and Bryan Robson (England); Arthur Albiston and Gordon Strachan (Scotland); Norman Whiteside (N. Ireland); John Sivebaek and Jesper Olsen (Denmark)

QUIZ 24
WORLD CUP – PAST HISTORY

1. Brazil
2. Argentina
3. Paolo Rossi
4. Portugal
5. Johan Cruyff
6. 0-0

7. Carlos Alberto
8. The 1982 tournament
9. Jimmy Greaves
10. 1990
11. Paul Breitner
12. Jairzinho (Brazil)

13. 1950
14. Italy
15. Rene van de Kerkhof
16. 1970
17. England and Brazil
18. 'Bulldog Bobby'

Sharp in the Box
Czechoslovakia, Hungary, Sweden, West Germany
Italy and Holland

QUIZ 25
THE MANAGERS

1. Bruce Rioch
2. Oldham
3. Dave Bassett
4. Andy Roxburgh
5. Alex Ferguson
6. Ossie Ardiles and Alan Ball

7. The Czech Republic (Dusan Uhrin)
8. QPR
9. Notts County
10. Goalkeeper
11. Neil Warnock
12. Kevin Keegan

13. Matt Busby
14. Alan Mullery
15. Glenn Helder
16. Jimmy Nicholl
17. Eoin Hand
18. Southampton

Sharp in the Box
Lincoln City, Watford, Aston Villa and Wolves

QUIZ 26
HAVE BOOTS WILL TRAVEL

1. Norwich
2. Paul Gascoigne
3. Arsenal
4. David Platt
5. Alan Ball
6. Mo Johnston

7. Paul Peschisolido
8. Northern Ireland
9. Nigel Spackman
10. Carlton Palmer and Nigel Worthington
11. Derby
12. Gillingham and Norwich

13. Spurs
14. Steve Daley
15. 15
16. Huddersfield Town
17. Gordon Smith
18. Burnley

Sharp in the Box
Coventry, Portsmouth, Rangers, QPR and Leeds

QUIZ 27
THE FOREIGN LEGION

1. Leeds and Manchester United
2. Gianluca Vialli
3. Wolves
4. Jan Molby
5. Newcastle
6. German

7. West Ham's Steve Potts
8. Mixu Paatelainen
9. Birmingham City
10. Gica Popescu
11. Bert Trautmann
12. Frans Thijssen

13. Czechoslovakia's
14. Anfield, Liverpool
15. He was one of the two Argentinians sent off in the World Cup Final
16. Ceri Evans
17. Preben Arentoft
18. Max Seeburg

Sharp in the Box
Craig Johnston and Bruce Grobbelaar

Quiz 28
EARLY EXCHANGES

1. Bryan Robson
2. France
3. San Marino
4. Vinnie Jones
5. Chris Sutton
6. Four seconds

7. Liam O'Brien
8. Steve Bould
9. Newcastle
10. Bryan Robson
11. Jack Taylor
12. Argentina (v Greece)

13. Australia
14. Ten seconds
15. Johnny Rep
16. Rangers and Hearts
17. Tommy Lawton
18. Nandor Hidegkuti

Sharp in the Box
Italy, West Germany (twice), Brazil (twice) and England

QUIZ 29
YOU ARE THE REF

1. Yes
2. Goalkeepers
3. Yes, but only if the ball has touched another player (e.g. the goalkeeper) before he strikes it again
4. Ten
5. No
6. 12 yards

7. False, there is no limit
8. There is no signal for a direct free-kick, only for an indirect one
9. 16 ounces
10. The referee is unlikely to allow this since it constitutes an unnecessary danger to opponents
11. False, the other players need only be outside the penalty-area
12. At the half-way line

13. A direct free-kick from the place where the attacker was standing
14. No, they must be white
15. Yes, any player may change places with the goalkeeper providing the referee is informed and the game is stopped
16. No, unless he considers that there was an attempt to deceive an opponent
17. 130 yards
18. Law 17 (corner-kick)

Sharp in the Box
Handling the ball plus striking, holding or pushing
an opponent

Quiz 30
4-3-3

1. Mark Hughes
2. Bristol City
3. Pele
4. Barcelona
5. The League Championship, the Milk (League) Cup and the European Cup
6. Wallace

7. Emilio Butragueno
8. Livingston (formerly Meadowbank Thistle)
9. Denis Law, Bobby Charlton and George Best
10. Crystal Palace
11. Cameroon and Italy
12. Bayern Munich, Borussia Moenchengladbach and Hamburg SV

13. Stranraer
14. Tony Adcock, Paul Stewart and David White
15. 1981
16. Neuchatel Xamax
17. 1977
18. Alfredo di Stefano

Sharp in the Box
George Cohen, Jack Charlton, Bobby Moore
and Ray Wilson

QUIZ 31
DRAMATIC DEBUTS

1. Alan Shearer
2. Bryan Roy
3. Graeme Souness
4. No
5. Jimmy Greaves
6. True, he netted with a header

7. Six
8. Denis Law
9. Arsenal
10. Mark Hughes
11. Tony Coton
12. Swindon Town

13. Leicester
14. Six seconds
15. Billy Dodds
16. Paul Goddard
17. Torino
18. Allan Clarke (1970)

Sharp in the Box
Dalian Atkinson, Cyrille Regis and Steve Staunton

Quiz 32
Super Subs

1. Ronnie Rosenthal
2. Ian Rush
3. Stuart McCall
4. Roger Milla
5. Crystal Palace
6. One of the goal-frames had to be replaced

7. Mark Robins
8. Arsenal
9. 1982 (Altobelli of Italy)
10. David Fairclough
11. George Graham
12. Joe Jordan

13. Ralph Coates
14. Albania
15. Dick Nanninga (for Holland in 1978)
16. John Hewitt
17. Alan Fettis
18. Hungary

Sharp in the Box
a) 1965 b) 1987

QUIZ 33
QUITE A SEASON – 1995-96

1. Paul Gascoigne
2. Peter Schmeichel
3. A judgement by the European Court of Justice which declared that football's transfer system and UEFA's 'three foreigners' rule were illegal
4. Liverpool
5. Wimbledon
6. Anfield

7. Colombia's Rene Higuita
8. Blackburn
9. South Africa
10. Ian Rush
11. Barry Venison
12. Peter Beardsley

13. Willem II
14. Stevenage Borough
15. Diego Maradona and Eric Cantona
16. York City
17. *When Saturday Comes*
18. Because of a pitch invasion

Sharp in the Box
Switzerland, Bulgaria and Hungary

QUIZ 34
ROUND THE GROUNDS

1. Stamford Bridge
2. Manchester City
3. Hampden Park
4. Charlton Athletic
5. Wembley
6. False, there is a nearby cricket ground of the same name

7. Berwick Rangers
8. Wimbledon
9. Portman Road
10. Cleethorpes
11. The Pontiac Silverdome
12. Middlesbrough, because their own ground had been closed due to the club's financial difficulties

13. Selhurst Park
14. The Olympic Stadium, Munich
15. They are all named after an individual
16. West Ham's
17. Wigan Athletic
18. Sixfields Stadium

Sharp in the Box
Ibrox (1961), Hampden Park (1960, 1966 and 1976)
and Tannadice (1987)

QUIZ 35
QUITE A SEASON – 1994-95

1. Paul Ince
2. Ian Wright
3. Alan Shearer
4. The Scottish Cup
5. Bobby Robson
6. Eric Cantona

7. Georgia
8. Robert Lee
9. The 'Young Player of the Year'
10. 2-0 to Milan
11. He became the third man to manage two different clubs to League Championship success
12. Trabzonspor

13. Blackpool
14. Stefan Schwarz
15. Kevin Campbell
16. Vinnie Jones
17. Forfar Athletic
18. Because the ground of Conference winners Macclesfield was not considered to be up to Football League standard

---

Sharp in the Box
Amokachi and Ferguson (Everton), Giggs and
Scholes (Manchester United)

QUIZ 36
ON THE SPOT

1. Gareth Southgate
2. On the goal-line between the posts
3. Diana Ross
4. Genoa (v Sampdoria)
5. Paul McStay
6. Chris Waddle and Stuart Pearce

7. Gianfranco Zola
8. Liverpool
9. Four
10. Sheffield Wednesday
11. Kevin Reeves
12. Luton's Andy Dibble

13. All fifteen
14. The penalty-spot had been obliterated and so the groundsman had to measure out and paint a new one
15. Robbie Rensenbrink
16. Tony Parks
17. Andy Brehme
18. 20-19

Sharp in the Box
Shearer, Platt, Pearce, Gascoigne and Sheringham

Quiz 37
Quite a Season – 1993-94

1. Andy Cole
2. Mark Hateley
3. Paul Gascoigne
4. Marseille
5. Francis Lee
6. One

7. They conceded 100 Premiership goals
8. Notts County
9. Tranmere Rovers
10. Torino and Parma
11. Denmark
12. Alan Shearer

13. For the first time ever, it comprised solely Rangers fans
14. Brian Talbot
15. The FA feared crowd trouble because the match fell on Hitler's birthday
16. Nigeria
17. Wimbledon owner Sam Hammam
18. Manchester

Sharp in the Box
Eddie Newton and Frank Sinclair

QUIZ 38
RECORD BREAKERS

1. Andy Cole
2. Kenny Dalglish
3. Sheffield Wednesday
4. Norman Whiteside
5. Manchester United
6. Walter Zenga

7. Coventry City
8. Kevin Francis
9. Gordon Strachan
10. 13
11. Pat Jennings
12. Dumbarton

13. Dixie Dean
14. 101
15. Austria v Hungary
16. Southend (with seven successive penalty misses)
17. Maine Road
18. Pele

Sharp in the Box
Alf Common, David Jack and Denis Law

Quiz 39
Quite a Season – 1992-93

1. Leeds and Rangers
2. Brian Clough
3. Arsenal v Spurs and Sheffield Wednesday v Sheffield United
4. Vinnie Jones
5. Birmingham City
6. Peter Beardsley

7. None
8. Steve Coppell
9. Poland
10. Paul McGrath
11. Guy Whittingham
12. Lisbon

13. Cwmbran Town
14. Jason Livingstone
15. San Marino
16. Stuttgart had breached UEFA regulations by using one foreign player too many in the second leg match
17. Les Ferdinand
18. Six

Sharp in the Box
Arsenal's Steve Morrow, who collected his winners' medal from the Coca-Cola Cup Final. He had been unable to receive it at the time because of an injury sustained during the post-match celebrations.

QUIZ 40
SOCCER – THE WORLD GAME

1. The J.League
2. Zambia
3. Coventry City
4. The World Club Championship match
5. North Korea
6. Pele

7. The Copa America
8. Ecuador
9. China
10. 1982
11. Velez Sarsfield
12. Yokohama

13. Flamengo and Fluminense
14. Ghana
15. Qatar
16. FAR
17. Colombia
18. Tony Waiters

Sharp in the Box
Saudi Arabia and South Korea

QUIZ 41
THE CHAMPIONS' CUP

1. Manchester United
2. Rome
3. Barcelona and PSV Eindhoven
4. Chris Waddle
5. AEK Athens
6. Rome

7. Marcel Desailly
8. 1987 (Bayern Munich v Porto)
9. Vujadin Boskov
10. Benfica
11. Trevor Francis
12. Bayern Munich (1974)

13. Patrick Kluivert
14. Miodrag Belodedic
15. Ernst Happel
16. Spartak Moscow
17. Karl-Marx-Stadt
18. Ferenc Puskas (Real Madrid v Benfica, 1962)

Sharp in the Box
AC Milan, Manchester United, Ajax, Liverpool
and Barcelona

QUIZ 42
FUTBOL ESPANOL

1. Atletico Madrid
2. Johan Cruyff
3. Real Zaragoza
4. Red
5. John Toshack
6. The Nou Camp

7. Gheorghe Hagi
8. Tenerife
9. Real Sociedad
10. Andoni Zubizarreta
11. Chamartin
12. Deportivo La Coruna

13. Real Oviedo
14. Valencia
15. Abel Resino
16. Seville
17. Luis Suarez
18. The Spanish First Division's leading goalscorer

Sharp in the Box
Barcelona, Real Madrid and Atletico Madrid

QUIZ 43
STARS OF EUROPE

1. Lothar Matthaus
2. Ajax
3. Hristo Stoichkov
4. Portugal
5. Franco Baresi
6. 1984

7. Michel Preud'homme
8. Denis Law
9. Yordan Lechkov
10. The Czech Republic
11. Alessandro Costacurta
12. Eric Gerets

13. Heinz Hermann
14. Hamburg
15. Montenegro
16. Finn Laudrup
17. Rudi Krol
18. Greece

Sharp in the Box
Gerd Muller, Franz Beckenbauer, Karl-Heinz Rummenigge
and Lothar Matthaus

QUIZ 44
THE CUP-WINNERS' CUP

1. Nayim
2. Brussels
3. Alex Ferguson
4. Mark Hughes
5. Ajax
6. Gianluca Vialli

7. Werder Bremen
8. Barcelona
9. Wynton Rufer
10. Feyenoord
11. Anderlecht
12. Atletico Madrid

13. Wolves
14. Dinamo Batumi
15. Nine
16. West Ham
17. Anderlecht, in 1978
18. 10-1 to Monaco

Sharp in the Box
Andy Gray, Trevor Steven and Kevin Sheedy

QUIZ 45
CALCIO – THE ITALIAN LEAGUE

1. Juventus
2. Inter Milan
3. Rome
4. Mauve and white
5. Milan
6. Foreign players

7. Alexi Lalas
8. The League Champions and the Italian Cup holders
9. Igor Protti (Bari)
10. They became the first team to win the Championship without losing a match
11. Pietro Vierchowod
12. Giovanni Trapattoni

13. Cagliari
14. Gordon Cowans and Paul Rideout
15. Genoa
16. AC Milan's
17. Three (Torino, Juventus and Napoli)
18. He was their goalkeeper, having ventured upfield for a last-minute corner

---

Sharp in the Box
Fiorentina, AC Milan, Inter Milan, Juventus,
Roma and Sampdoria

QUIZ 46
THE UEFA CUP

1. Bayern Munich
2. Nottingham Forest
3. It is played over two 'home-and-away' legs
4. Ipswich and Spurs
5. Dundee United
6. Bordeaux

7. Fabrizio Ravanelli
8. IFK Gothenburg
9. Bill Shankly
10. Odense
11. VfB Stuttgart
12. John Wark (Ipswich)

13. The International Inter-City Industrial Fairs Cup
14. Jeremy Goss
15. Bayer Leverkusen
16. Mike Belfield
17. Real Madrid (1985 and 1986)
18. Juventus (they lost the Final to Leeds on 'away goals')

Sharp in the Box
Ajax, Barcelona, Bayern Munich and Juventus

QUIZ 47
THE FRENCH CONNECTION

1. Nantes
2. The Parc des Princes, Paris
3. Eric Cantona
4. Olympique Marseille
5. The Cup-Winners' Cup
6. Basile Boli

7. Auxerre
8. Saint-Etienne
9. 'Straight to goal'
10. Bastia
11. 1988
12. Montpellier

13. Raymond Goethals
14. Roger
15. Metz
16. Manual Amoros
17. He revealed that Marseille officials had tried to bribe him to throw a league match
18. The Stade Louis II in Monaco

Sharp in the Box
Stade de Reims, Saint-Etienne and Marseille

QUIZ 48
CONTINENTAL HIT-MEN

1. Adidas
2. George Weah
3. *'Der Bomber'*
4. Switzerland
5. Jean-Pierre Papin
6. Marseille

7. Ajax
8. CSKA Sofia
9. Oleg Salenko
10. Seville
11. Jan Ceulemans
12. Stefan Pettersson

13. Ulf Kirsten (Leverkusen) and Ronaldo (PSV)
14. Mozambique
15. Kennet Andersson (Sweden)
16. Toni Polster
17. Tanju Colak
18. It was revealed that he had been a spy for the *Stasi* (secret police) under the old East German regime

---

Sharp in the Box
Bobby Lennox, Joe Harper and Charlie Nicholas

Quiz 49
Sporting Soccer Fans

1. Barry Hearn
2. Boris Becker
3. Liz McColgan
4. Seve Ballesteros
5. Steve Cram
6. Stephen Hendry

7. Crystal Palace
8. Graham Gooch
9. Coventry City
10. Charlton
11. Chelsea
12. Julian Wilson

13. Wolves
14. Jonathan Davies
15. Celtic
16. Andy Gregory
17. Leeds
18. John McCririck

Sharp in the Box
Robbie Brightwell and Ann Packer

QUIZ 50
READ ALL ABOUT IT

1. *Shoot!*
2. *Fever Pitch*
3. Arsenal
4. Germany
5. Jimmy Greaves
6. Goalkeepers

7. *Viz*
8. *Rangers News*
9. Brian Glanville
10. Walter Smith
11. Bobby Robson's
12. Spain

13. Spurs in European competition
14. Charles Hughes
15. Port Vale
16. Arsenal's Irish players
17. *La Gazzetta dello Sport*
18. *Hampden Babylon*

Sharp in the Box
It's a play on words referring to the fans' song 'Wen…dy
Saints, go marching in…'

QUIZ 51
HOWZAT!
FOOTBALLING CRICKETERS

1. Viv Richards
2. Andy Goram
3. Scunthorpe United
4. Geoff Hurst
5. Mike Gatting
6. The Oval

7. Denis Compton
8. Jim Cumbes
9. Brian Close
10. Ted Drake
11. Bramall Lane (home of Sheffield United)
12. Phil

13. Charlton
14. Phil Neale
15. Scot Symon
16. Chris Balderstone
17. Tim Buzaglo
18. Hamilton Crescent

Sharp in the Box
In olden days, a bowler who took three consecutive
wickets was rewarded with a new hat

Quiz 52
The Colours

1. Red
2. Claret and blue
3. Blackburn Rovers
4. Grey
5. A large red panel down front and back
6. Hibs and Celtic

7. Leeds
8. He turned his jersey round back-to-front
9. Umbro
10. A red-and-white chequered pattern
11. Arsenal's
12. Black and white

13. Coventry
14. Four
15. Albion Rovers
16. They wore white jerseys in the first half and (on the instructions of the referee) blue in the second
17. White, green and black
18. Swapping jerseys

Sharp in the Box
White, red, yellow, sky blue and indigo (although most people considered that latest strip to be grey!)

QUIZ 53
YOU MUST BE JOKING!

1. Bill Shankly
2. Vinnie Jones
3. Graham Taylor
4. The referee booked him!
5. The story of John Major's son who had been sent off for the fourth time in a season while playing for his school team
6. Jasper Carrott

7. Stan Boardman
8. Jan Molby
9. John Aldridge
10. Hampden Park
11. 39-year-old Ray Wilkins
12. Mick McCarthy

13. Dave Bassett
14. 'See one wall and you've seen them all'
15. Jimmy Greaves
16. He said that it would ruin his Saturday nights
17. John Motson
18. Alex Ferguson

Sharp in the Box
Tommy Docherty

QUIZ 54
THE SONG REMAINS THE SAME

1. 'You'll Never Walk Alone'
2. David Baddiel and Frank Skinner
3. Luciano Pavarotti
4. 'Abide With Me'
5. West Ham's
6. Ossie Ardiles

7. 'Elland Road is the only place for us'
8. Portsmouth's
9. 'Guantanamera'
10. 'Gloryland'
11. Eric Idle
12. 'Goodnight Irene'

13. 'Cheer Up Peter Reid'
14. Manchester City
15. Celtic's
16. He's a Manchester United fan
17. 'Careless Hands'
18. John Robertson

Sharp in the Box
Steve Archibald

QUIZ 55
SOCCER ON THE BOX

1. *Match of the Day*
2. Trevor Brooking
3. Graham Taylor
4. Arsenal
5. Kenneth Wolstenholme's
6. ITV

7. Martin Tyler
8. Kevin Keegan
9. 'Statto'
10. Ian Botham (he played football too, remember!)
11. Barry Davies
12. Wycombe Wanderers

13. 1954
14. Simon O'Brien
15. Boston United
16. Jock Brown
17. Michael Robinson
18. Don Howe

Sharp in the Box
Dundee United, Aston Villa, Wolves, Everton,
Notts County, West Bromwich and Rangers

Quiz 56
Strange But True?

1. True (Allan Hansen of Odense BK)
2. Kenny Dalglish
3. True (Richard Gough)
4. Everton
5. True (Princess Alexandra, wife of Edward VII)
6. Uri Geller

7. Stan Bowles
8. That year's competition was played on a two-leg basis
9. Both ties were played in their shared stadium
10. Malta
11. Alex Stepney
12. Vic Halom

13. Seven
14. Their head of state had threatened to execute them if they played badly!
15. Cowdenbeath
16. Swindon
17. Because the club was founded by two Blackburn Rovers fans
18. A dog which ran onto the field and tackled him

Sharp in the Box
Neville Southall (1985), Clive Allen (1987)
and John Barnes (1988)

Quiz 57
Go For The Century

1. Wimbledon
2. Carlsberg
3. Blackpool
4. The Intertoto Cup
5. Faustino Asprilla
6. Brighton
7. Paris Saint-Germain
8. Tottenham
9. Torquay
10. Chris Waddle

11. Burnley
12. Martin O'Neill
13. Paul Ince
14. Barcelona
15. Colin Cooper
16. Birmingham City
17. Three
18. Gordon Strachan
19. Sheffield United
20. Carl

21. Kenny Dalglish
22. Macclesfield
23. Barry Davies
24. 2002
25. Dundee United
26. *Take Your Pick* host Des O'Connor at one time played for Northampton's youth team
27. Everton

28. Espanol
29. Eric Hall (Dennis Wise's agent who was aghast at the prison sentence imposed on the Chelsea skipper)
30. Hazel Irvine

31. 16
32. Paul Gascoigne
33. Geoff Hurst
34. Queen's Park
35. A back-flip
36. Uruguay
37. Watford
38. £1.5 million
39. Grimsby
40. The play-off finals

41. For refusing to have his hair cut
42. Norway
43. Exeter City
44. Yes
45. Bruce Grobbelaar and Steve McManaman
46. No.17
47. Galatasaray
48. West Bromwich Albion
49. Roy McFarland
50. Partick Thistle

51. A bakery
52. Eric Cantona
53. A dance troop which provided pre-match entertainment on Sky's *Monday Night Football* programme
54. Highbury
55. David Icke
56. Chris Bart-Williams
57. Liverpool

58. 'El Tel'
59. Ian Durrant
60. Lennie Lawrence

61. Wim Jonk
62. Norway
63. Australia
64. Green
65. Elland Road, Leeds
66. Trevor Francis
67. Molineux, Wolves
68. Billy Bremner
69. 'The Owls'
70. Preston

71. Oxford, in 1986
72. QPR's
73. Borussia Dortmund
74. Mike Summerbee
75. True
76. Andy King
77. Peru
78. Manchester United and Newcastle
79. Aberdeen
80. Gordon Durie

81. Newcastle
82. 1966
83. Wolves
84. The Republic of Ireland
85. Brian Laudrup
86. Manchester United
87. France
88. Safety at football grounds
89. Italy (Mancini) and Croatia (Boban)

90. Dundee

91. It's the type of wood from which the majority of goal-frames are made
92. £7 million
93. Joël
94. Crewe Alexandra
95. 'Animal'
96. Tony Yeboah
97. Honduras and El Salvador
98. Canon
99. Lee Chapman
100. Two